700
cutics

100

Twayne's English Authors Series

Sylvia E. Bowman, *Editor*

INDIANA UNIVERSITY

Richard Brinsley Sheridan

TEAS 183

Engraving by Hall after the portrait by Sir Joshua Reynolds

Richard Brinsley Sheridan

Richard Brinsley Sheridan

By JACK D. DURANT
North Carolina State University

TWAYNE PUBLISHERS

A DIVISION OF G. K. HALL & CO., BOSTON

Library of Congress Cataloging in Publication Data

Durant, Jack Davis, 1930 -
  Richard Brinsley Sheridan.

  (Twayne's English authors series; TEAS 183)
  Bibliography: pp. 157 - 60.
  Includes index.
  1.   Sheridan, Richard Brinsley Butler, 1751 - 1816.
I.   Title.
PR3683.D87   822'.6 [B]   75 - 1094
ISBN 0-8057-6650-2

MANUFACTURED IN THE UNITED STATES OF AMERICA

To the ever dear memory of
May May

Contents

About the Author

Jack D. Durant received his undergraduate degree in 1953 from Maryville College (Maryville, Tennessee). After receiving his M. A. degree (1955) from the University of Tennessee, Mr. Durant served for two years in Europe with the Third Armored Division, United States Army. He taught at Maryville College and Presbyterian College (Clinton, South Carolina) before continuing his graduate education, in 1960, at the University of Tennessee. Selected as one of three "University Fellows" in 1962, he received his Ph.D. degree from that university in 1963.

Mr. Durant has taught eighteenth-century studies, specializing in the novel and the drama, at both the undergraduate and graduate levels. He served on the faculty of Auburn University from 1963-71. Since 1971, he has taught at North Carolina State University where he has been Director of Graduate Studies in English.

The author has served as secretary-treasurer and chairman of the Southern Humanities Conference, as associate editor and business manager of the *Southern Humanities Review* and as program chairman for the English Literature (III) Section of the South Atlantic Modern Language Association. He has edited a collection of essays entitled *Religion as a Humanizing Force in Man's History — Past and Present,* essays presented in a symposium sponsored by the Southern Humanities Conference during his chairmanship in 1968-9. His published essays and reviews on *Beowulf* and modern writers, including Samuel Beckett, Stanley Berne, and B. Traven, as well as on Otway, Vanbrugh, Goldsmith, and Sheridan, have appeared in *Tennessee Studies in Literature, Southern Speech Communication Journal, Ball State University Forum, Studies in Short Fiction, South Atlantic Bulletin, Restoration and Eighteenth-Century Theatre Research,* and *Studies in Philology.* His current major research interest continues to be Sheridan.

Preface

This exposition of Richard Brinsley Sheridan's literary art and theory sketches so much of his life as bears closely upon his literary and theatrical careers. It does not argue a thesis; rather, it seeks to describe — in a roughly chronological-topical way — the range and quality of Sheridan's work, to construct formal backgrounds where they are apposite, to summarize and evaluate earlier criticism where it is available (and noteworthy), to offer new insights where possible, and to allow each topic to dictate through its own special properties the critical exposition most appropriate to it. This study does not debate unsettled attributions; it does not discuss clearly apocryphal titles; and, for want of adequate texts, it does not discuss Sheridan's speeches at great length. What is new it offers in relation to what is old; for, like other such surveys, it is somewhat derivative. It concedes of course that much yet remains to be said, especially about Sheridan's dramaturgy and about his ethical milieu. But no other book has thus far attempted a critical-analytical account of Sheridan's entire major canon, the poetry and the theory as well as the plays; and this book seeks to supply that need, offering itself as an introduction and a survey. Since it was completed before the appearance of *The Dramatic Works of Richard Brinsley Sheridan*, edited by Cecil Price (Oxford, 1973), the textual references cite the edition of R. Crompton Rhodes (Oxford, 1928), and the textual information derives chiefly from that source. Where Price's more recent findings and judgments relate to the exposition, I acknowledge them in the "Notes and References." In somewhat different form, short portions of Chapters 3, 4, and 6 have appeared earlier in *The Southern Speech Journal, The Ball State University Forum*, and *The South Atlantic Bulletin*.

At the outset, the Research Council of Auburn University voted me a generous grant-in-aid for research and travel, and of course I am grateful for that help. I am grateful, too, to Chancellor Sylvia Bowman, the editor of Twayne's English Authors Series, for many kinds of thoughtful assistance. To Professors Richard Amacher, Eugene Current-Garcia, Sara Hudson, David Jeffrey, and Barbara Mowat, my colleagues at Auburn University, I give thanks for unfailing wise counsel and good encouragement. I also thank Dr. Ruth Fourier, Mrs. Frances Honour, Mrs. Knox McMillan, and many others at the Ralph Brown Draughon Library (Auburn University) for helping me to secure rare sources and to solve frustrating problems of research. I am grateful to Mrs. Carl Rickard, Mrs. Sylvia Gurkin, and Mrs. Veronica Johnson for typing the manuscript and its numerous revisions. And of course I am grateful to my wife for her immeasurable patience and firm high hope.

I dedicate the book to my gentle daughter Mary, not certainly because it is worthy of her memory but because her tender constant presence warms my days.

JACK D. DURANT

North Carolina State University

Chronology

1751   Richard Brinsley Sheridan born in September or October at 12 Dorset Street, Dublin; christened "Thos. Brinsley" at St. Mary's Church, Dublin, on November 4.

1757   Enters Samuel Whyte's grammar school in Dublin.

≤1762   Enters Harrow School.

←1766   His mother, Frances Chamberlaine Sheridan, dies at Blois.

1768   Leaves Harrow to join his family in Soho (some biographers say 1769; others, 1767); studies under the direction of his father.

1770   Moves to Bath to assist in his father's new Academy of Oratory. Collaborates with Nathaniel Brassey Halhed to compose the burlesque burletta *Ixion*.

1771   Publishes satiric poems "The Ridotto of Bath" and "Clio's Protest"; translates and publishes (with Halhed) *The Love Epistles of Aristaenetus*.

1772   Elopes to the Continent with Elizabeth Linley (March); fights two duels with Miss Linley's admirer, Captain Thomas Mathews (May and July). Banished by his father to Farm Hill, Waltham Abbey, to recover from his wounds and to pursue random studies.

1773   Enrolls at Middle Temple (April 6); marries Elizabeth Linley (April 13); they take a house at East Burnham.

1774   Takes a house in Orchard Street. Publishes "A Familiar Epistle"; puts *The Rivals* into rehearsal (November).

1775   First performances of *The Rivals* (January 17), *St. Patrick's Day* (May 2), and *The Duenna* (November 21) all at Covent Garden Theatre. Son Thomas born (November 17).

1776   In partnership with James Ford and Thomas Linley, buys David Garrick's shares in Drury Lane Theatre, assuming management in September.

1777   First performances of *A Trip to Scarborough* (February 24) and *The School for Scandal* (May 8) at Drury Lane. Joins Literary Club (March).

1778   First performances of *The Camp* (October 15) at Drury Lane.

1779   First presentation of "Verses to the Memory of Garrick" (March 11); first performance of *The Critic* (October 30), both at Drury Lane.

1780   Elected member of Parliament for Stafford. Composes an interlude ("The Storming and Taking of Fort Omoa") for the pantomime *Harlequin Fortunatus*.

1781   Produces the pantomime *Robinson Crusoe; or Harlequin Friday*.

1782   Appointed Under-Secretary of State for the Northern Department.

1783   Appointed Secretary of the Treasury under Charles James Fox and Lord North.

1787   Speaks for the motion to impeach Warren Hastings (February 7).

1788   Speaks at the trial of Warren Hastings (June). Advises Prince George in the First Regency Crisis. His father, Thomas Sheridan, dies (September 26).

1789   Supports the French Revolution after the fall of the Bastille.

1790   Breaks with Edmund Burke over the issue of the French Revolution.

1791   Birth of his daughter Mary. Drury Lane closed for reconstruction.

1792   His wife dies (June 28); his infant daughter dies (October).

1794   Drury Lane reopens. Collaborates in composing *The Glorious First of June*, a musical afterpiece (July).

1795   Marries Hester Jane Ogle (April 27).

1796   Son Charles Brinsley born (January 14).

1797   Assists in resolving the naval mutinies at Spithead and the Nore (April and May). Revises *The Glorious First of June* (1794) and re-stages it as *Cape St. Vincent*.

1798   Revises Benjamin Thompson's translation of August von Kotzebue's *Menschenhass und Reue;* introduces it as *The Stranger* at Drury Lane (March 24).

1799   First production of *Pizarro* (May 24) adapted from Kotzebue's *Die Spanier in Peru*.

1802   Defeats the bill brought against him in Chancery Court by his creditors.

1804   Appointed Receiver General of the Duchy of Cornwall. Presents the boy actor William Henry West Betty to enthusiastic audiences at Drury Lane.

1806   Treasurer of the navy in the Ministry of All the Talents. Wins Parliamentary seat for Westminster after the death of Charles James Fox. Collaborates in operatic romance *The Forty Thieves*.

1807   Loses his seat for Westminster but is returned for Ilchester.

1809   Drury Lane Theatre burns (February 24). Re-establishes company at the Lyceum; asks Samuel Whitbread to manage the reconstruction.

1811   Advises Prince George in the Second Regency Crisis. Considers standing again for Stafford and assesses the support yet available to him there.

1812   Rejected by Stafford.

1813   Is imprisoned for debt (August); remains for three nights in the spunging house.

1814   Considers standing again for Westminster but withdraws.

1816   Dies at 17 Savile Row on Sunday July 7; buried in Westminster Abbey.

CHAPTER 1

Equal to Any Difficulty

WHEN Richard Sheridan wrote to his second wife on April 20, 1810, he aptly confessed the paradox of his own character. "No one," he wrote, "can be . . . of a more negligent forgetful and procrastinating habit of mind than I am, united at the same time with a most unfortunately sanguine temper, and a rash confidence that I am capable of exertions equal to any difficulty whenever extremity may call for them."[1] At twenty-four, certainly motivated by his "sanguine temper" and by his "rash confidence," he had negotiated to manage Drury Lane Theatre. At twenty-five, already distinguished as author of the "two best comedies of his age,"[2] he had won membership in the exclusive Literary Club. At twenty-nine, he had launched a Parliamentary career which continued for thirty-two years and achieved a brilliance only less lustrous than the careers of Edmund Burke and Charles James Fox. His three lives as writer, theater manager, and Parliamentarian virtually proved him "capable of exertions equal to any difficulty"; but, from the other half of his nature, from his monumental negligence and procrastination, he emerged in his own day a legend of indolence and improvidence. It was inevitable, and symbolically fitting, that the Sheridan at last borne away for burial in Westminster Abbey should die impoverished and desperate.[3]

The qualities of Sheridan's mature genius and of his personal failings relate with remarkable directness to his family backgrounds, his childhood and education. In character, certainly, he recalls his paternal grandfather, Thomas Sheridan, an Irish clergyman talented in his own rights as teacher, Classicist, linguist, musician, punster, and practical joker, but best known as the close friend of Jonathan Swift in Dublin. In grandfather and grandson, says Sheridan's most exhaustive biographer, appear "the same whimsical sense of deranged honour, the same dupability . . . the same sanguine carelessness and open-handed extravagance, the same struggles with debt and duns . . . the same vain absence of mind."[4] To Richard's father, his own son and namesake, Thomas Sheridan transmitted fine scholarly gifts and an active zeal for educational reforms. But the younger Thomas inherited little of his father's infectious joviality, little of his generosity and good nature. From the two Thomases, however, the whole Richard takes form. For, if the grandfather foreshadowed Richard's temperament, the father supplied a pattern for his diverse career.

When Richard was born at 12 Dorset Street, Dublin, sometime during the autumn of 1751,[5] his father prospered as manager of the Smock-Alley Theatre and enjoyed acclaim as Ireland's leading actor. Though his training at Westminster School and at Trinity College, Dublin, had prepared him for clerical orders and for teaching, he had chosen the stage as promising more money and as gratifying at the same time his love for language and reform. Bringing to the theater a scholar's taste for Classical form and an orator's flair for declamation, he had captured the enthusiasm of the Irish audiences as had no one before him, and he was favored in Dublin even over James Quin and David Garrick. But prosperity smiled on the Sheridans only until 1754; for then, on March 2, a political riot virtually destroyed the Smock-Alley Theatre and consequently beggared the family. In 1756, after two lean years in London, Thomas returned with his family to make peace with the Dublin audience and to promote a grand educational scheme, "The Hibernian Academy."

But, just as he could not restore his earlier popularity as an actor, neither could he convince his countrymen to accept him as a progressive educator. He therefore left Ireland again in 1758 to take lodgings for his family in London. Thirty years remained to him, years variously given to linguistic and elocutionary projects. For his scholarship he won significant honors — master's degrees from Oxford and Cambridge, a pension of two-hundred pounds from the Crown, the freedom of the city of Edinburgh — but never again was his family to enjoy the security of the Smock-Alley Theatre days. Certainly his father's vanity and prodigality robbed the young Richard of every real sense of stability, just as his persistent interests in language, oratory, and the theater made clear marks upon the mature Richard's own theatrical and Parliamentary achievements.

In his college days, Thomas Sheridan had written a highly successful farce called *Captain O'Blunder: or The Brave Irishman* (introduced at Smock-Alley in 1743). But Richard's gifts as a dramatist relate less to his father's talents than to his mother's. The first of Frances Sheridan's plays, *The Discovery* (introduced at Drury Lane on February 5, 1763), was said by Garrick to be "one of the best comedies he ever read."[6] One performance of a second comedy, *The Dupe*, was staged at Drury Lane in December of 1763. And, though a third comedy, *A Journey to Bath*, was neither acted nor published until 1902, it may have suggested to Richard some details for his own later characterization of Mrs. Malaprop in *The Rivals*. In addition to the plays, Mrs. Sheridan authored three noteworthy prose romances — *Eugenia and Adelaide* (1739), *Memoirs of Sidney Bidulph* (1761), and *The History of Nourjahad* (1767) — and with one of them, *Sidney Bidulph*, she stormed the London literary world, winning the special plaudits of Samuel Richardson and Dr. Samuel Johnson. Charles James Fox, Richard's Parliamentary colleague in later years, thought it "the best novel in the English language."[7]

Until 1757, when Richard and his older brother Charles entered Samuel Whyte's grammar school in Dublin, the gentle and gifted Frances Sheridan had been their only tutor. She had recommended them to their new schoolmaster as "impenetrable dunces," and the record fairly supports her view. For Richard was certainly never to distinguish himself as a scholar, though his instructors at Harrow were to see in him "vestiges of a superior intellect."[8] The Harrow years — from 1762 to 1768 or 1769 — bred bitter memories for Richard. By his own account, he was often low spirited at school and "much given to crying when alone."[9] In 1764, the family, trying to retrench, had moved to Blois, where Frances Sheridan died two years later. Richard, meanwhile, remained a penniless, homeless, and melancholy inmate at Harrow; for he was neglected by his father. And so he continued until sometime during "his seventeenth year,"[10] when he rejoined his family, now resettled in London, to pursue his studies under his father's personal guidance. He took mathematics under Lewis Ker, a London physician; fencing and riding under Domenick Angelo, proprietor of a fencing and riding academy in Soho; and English rhetoric under Thomas Sheridan himself, after his own grand educational scheme.

Late in 1770, this grand scheme took the family to Bath, where Richard and Charles were to serve as rhetorical ushers in their father's new Academy of Oratory. By Richard's own testimony, the academy was "speedily laughed off the stage";[11] but Bath itself set the scene for exciting and romantic events, all of which figure subtly in the young playwright's art: his elopement with Elizabeth Linley and his two duels with Captain Thomas Mathews.

Elizabeth, a singer of oratorios in Bath, was perhaps the most celebrated soprano of her day and certainly one of the most celebrated beauties. When Richard met her, she was seventeen and a soloist for Thomas Sheridan's elocutionary vaudeville acts, his "Attic Entertainments," which featured lectures on elocution by Thomas himself and musical interludes by Miss Linley. Soon after the Sheridans arrived in Bath, Elizabeth had contracted to marry a sixty-year-old Wiltshire squire named Walter Long. But, for reasons not clearly known, Long had dissolved the contract; had settled three thousand pounds upon Elizabeth's father, who was director of oratorios in Bath; and had consigned to Elizabeth herself jewelry and other valuables worth over a thousand pounds. So widely publicized was the episode that Samuel Foote based a comedy on it, *The Maid of Bath,* allegorizing Elizabeth as the wronged innocent Kitty Linnet and Long as the ridiculous lecher Solomon Flint.

The succeeding months held additional embarrassments for Elizabeth. Captain Thomas Mathews, a married man and something of an intimate of the Linley family, began forcing his addresses upon her; at first, he threatened to kill himself if she refused him; then, on second thought, he threatened to ruin her reputation if he could not ruin her virtue. She confided her distress to Richard and decided, probably at his advice, to elope with him to France, where she might remain in a convent until Mathews stopped annoying her. It must have occurred to them on the way that the elopement itself could sully her reputation, for a reliable tradition holds that they were married — in name only — at a village near Calais.[12] They had left England near the end of March, 1772, and Elizabeth was soon after settled in a convent at Lille.

By the end of April, they were back in England. But, during their absence, Captain Mathews, feeling his honor assailed by a letter left behind in Bath by Richard, had publicly posted "Mr. Richard S-------" a "L---, and a treacherous S--------."[13] Two duels resulted. The first, at the Castle Tavern in Covent Garden, on May 4, 1772, was unsatisfactory because Mathews revoked the apology forced from him in the encounter. Richard had thoroughly bested him, broken his sword, and required him to beg his life. But Mathews afterwards insisted that to break the sword was to violate all received codes of practice and consequently to cancel the terms of the duel. He therefore called for a second meeting; and in this duel, staged on Kingsdown near Bath in the early dawn of July 1, 1772, Richard was defeated and wounded. Thrown to the ground and disarmed, he refused to beg his life; and on attempting to regain his defenses, he was stabbed repeatedly in the neck and chest by the dagger-like point of Mathews' sword which had broken from its hilt during the *mêlée*. Mathews then immediately fled to France, and poor Richard was taken to Bath to recover his health. Months later, as he languished on a farm near Waltham Abbey (under orders to forget Elizabeth Linley), he longed passionately for yet another meeting with Mathews. To his mind, the issue was never really settled.

But Elizabeth remained true to him; and on April 13, 1773, against their fathers' wishes they were married publicly at Marylebone Church. Since Richard would not hear of his wife's continuing in public life, he faced at once the necessity of building a career. And, as he developed himself as a man of letters, he clearly recalled the experiences of his recent past: the duels, the elopements, the sentimental courtships, the surly and absolutist parents. Many moments in his greatest comedies reflect the romantic adventures of his own young life as reshaped and relived in his comic imagination.

I Man of Letters

Even at Harrow he had laid a rude groundwork for his literary career. There he had attempted a dramatization of Oliver Goldsmith's *Vicar of Wakefield* and had shown in it an early feel for sharp dialogue and sentimental villainy. (His Thornhill vaguely anticipates Joseph Surface.)[14] And, between 1769 and 1772, he undertook a wide variety of literary projects, most of them left unfinished among his papers and some known only through letters from his friend Nathaniel Halhed, with whom he had translated from Theocritus in Harrow days. Work left among his papers includes two political satires: an ironic "defense" of Augustus, Duke of Grafton, somewhat in the manner of Swift, and a searing attack in the manner of Junius against one "Novus," a harsh critic in the public press of Grafton's successor to the prime ministry, Lord North.[15] Other prose remnants find the young satirist lampooning natural philosophy, in an "Epistle from a Cauliflower to Christopher Anstey, Esqr," and rejecting transmigrational Spiritualism, in an "Apology to Mr. Artichoke." In two quite sober pieces, both fragmentary, he attempted an essay on versification and a high-sounding treatise on "Patriotism" in which he defines patriotism as "a benevolent hope for the welfare of the society to which we belong." And Halhed's letters refer indirectly to yet a third treatise, a "new plan" to write about ancient and modern pastoral poetry.

Sheridan's half of the correspondence with Halhed is now lost; but Halhed's half, which dates between August, 1770, and October, 1771, hints at two other of young Sheridan's projects, a series of epigrams and a collection of "Crazy Tales"; and, of course, Halhed touches often upon his own collaborations with Sheridan. Together they wrote a burlesque burletta called *Ixion*, which was possibly submitted for production, though never staged. They also projected a periodical called "Hernan's Miscellany," a weekly series of commentaries upon the age as given by "Fred Hernan," whose qualifications as social observer, literary zealot, and critic of manners well equipped him for his role as reformer. Sheridan, who wrote the only known number of the "Miscellany," composed it in a freely associative Sterne-like style and neatly copied it out for the publisher; but it was never published. In fact, the only work of the young collaborators ever to see print was *The Love Epistles of Aristaenetus*, a series of loose translations from the Greek of an obscure ancient poetaster. Like Sheridan's own light verse satires, "Clio's Protest" and "The Ridotto of Bath," this work appeared in 1771.

Between 1770 and 1772, the love-struck Sheridan wrote many sweet anacreontics to his dear Eliza. He wrote yet others during his exile to Waltham Abbey. But, while there, he also undertook a bit of serious studying, on the inducement that he had "nothing else to do."[16] According to Walter Sichel, he worked problems in astronomy and mathematics and drilled himself in French and Italian. He sketched out an ambitious abstract of the history of England and filled several copy books with notes on geography, Latin, and horticulture.[17] During these years, too, he maintained a valuable correspondence with Thomas Grenville, a friend from Bath days and afterwards a colleague in Parliament, to whom he wrote long essay-like letters on such topics as friendship, the life of involvement as preferred to the life of retirement, and the philosophic acceptance of disappointed love. He also reflected a bit to Grenville about his reading, how he much preferred Sir Philip Sidney's *Arcadia* to the novels of Henry Fielding and Tobias Smollett because he favored life as it should be over life in a "vicious and corrupt society." And he promised to show his friend "some idle things" he had written.[18]

Sheridan had written some "Memoirs" (now lost) of his tempestuous affair with Miss Linley. But by these "idle things" he probably meant a series of disjointed strictures upon the style of Sir William Temple and a rather long rough commentary (seven pages of foolscap) on Blackstone's legal theories.[19] His complaints against Temple emphasize superfluous diction, awkward idiom, and ineffective metaphors. His comments on Blackstone declare that, since nature is law, "Society did not make Laws, but only confirmed what before existed" in nature. By extension of this logic, he also concludes that the only "possible state of Society possessing true Liberty" exists when all people are "exactly equal in Wealth, Possessions, etc., and agreed to abide by such and such convenants."[20] Consequently, "all laws at present are Tyranny." Such bold reassessments of the law properly enough engaged the interest of a young aspirant to the Middle Temple, where Sheridan enrolled on April 6, 1773; and the Waltham Abbey exile was at last ended.[21]

Just one week later he married Elizabeth Linley and took her to a honeymoon cottage in East Burnham. That autumn they moved into town, first living at the home of friends, Stephen Storace and his sister, then by February moving into their own house on Orchard Street, where Elizabeth's musicales quickly attracted a fashionable and select society. During the East Burnham and Orchard Street periods (1773 - 75), Richard continued to write, sharpening his political and literary interests, bidding for recognition through bold humanitarian projects. The boldest such project, a fragment, urges the Queen to establish a "Royal Sanctuary" to educate young women of gentle birth. Since women always exercise strong influence over men, Sheridan argues, they should certainly be educated to meet the responsibilities of moral and social leadership. The piece outlines a curriculum echoing Sheridan's distaste for novels and recommending basic studies in science, geography, home economics, and modern language. Its feminist argument directly recalls Mrs. Sullen's lamentation against English anti-feminism in Act II of George Farquhar's *The Beaux' Stratagem;* and the little work thus attests, as Sichel notes, young Sheridan's close knowledge of Farquhar.[22]

Again writing as a humanitarian, he jotted a few notes on Lord Chesterfield's letters to his natural son, letters published in 1774. These notes especially deplore the heartless competitiveness encouraged by the letters and their insistence on absolute parental authority. As a political theorist, Sheridan roughed a reply to Dr. Johnson's "Taxation No Tyranny" (1775), in which he rejected as hostile to political progress Johnson's view that mere birth in the realm implies tacit consent to the crown. He considers Johnson's pamphlet "trifling and insincere" like the "venal quit-rent of a birth-day ode," and he emphatically denies the Johnsonian theory that America must continue to be England's by right of conquest: "Right of Conquest necessarily ceases when the greater ceases to be the stronger, for it can then give no Protection to the weaker and consequently has no right to rule it."[23] Already he championed the American cause.

In other political writing, he composed a critique on the "flying piece of a political writer" about Lord North's ministry, directing his strictures chiefly against his opponent's diction and phrasing. This same derisive strategy characterizes his "Familiar Epistle," a lively verse satire attacking the arrogant claims of William Mason, who in a "Heroic Epistle" saw his own verse satire as stimulating important political reforms. Satire can hardly reform anything, Sheridan insists, and certainly not such badly executed satire as Mason's. The "Familiar Epistle," probably written in 1774, demonstrates by close reference to Mason's work just how bad a satirist Mason really is.

During the East Burnham and Orchard Street periods, Sheridan apparently thought also of starting a periodical paper to be called "The Detector" or "Dramatic Censor." Thomas Moore mentions seeing "some commencements" of such a project.[24] But, of course, the crowning achievement of these years is *The Rivals*, which took shape during the summer and fall of 1774 and appeared on the stage in January, 1775. As an aspiring dramatist, Sheridan had by now sketched discrete scenes for a fantasy, "A Wild Drama"; and he had possibly drawn up a "Pump Room Scene" vaguely figuring in the backgrounds of *The School for Scandal*. But *The Rivals* proved the vehicle of the moment. Gathering ideas from his letters to Grenville, from his "Royal Sanctuary," perhaps even from his notes on Chesterfield's letters, and drawing upon his current interest in (and tentative efforts at) dramatic writing, this comedy caught and contained the diverse play of his imagination and sped him on to fame. Soon after came *St. Patrick's Day*, a farce, and *The Duenna*, a comic opera (both 1775); and on March 14, 1777, two months before *The School for Scandal* appeared, he was elected, with Dr. Johnson's own nomination, a member of the exclusive Literary Club. "He who has written the two best comedies of his age," said Johnson, "is surely a considerable man."

II *Theatrical Manager*

In January, 1776, a good year before Sheridan joined the Literary Club, he had entered negotiations to buy David Garrick's half of the Drury Lane patent. By terms of the final agreement, which was concluded in June, Garrick's shares went to three partners, R. B. Sheridan, Thomas Linley, and James Ford. At five-thousand pounds a share, Sheridan and Linley each bought two shares; and Ford bought three. The other half of the patent remained in possession of Garrick's partner, Willoughby Lacy; and it continued to be encumbered by a mortgage of twenty-two-thousand pounds, which Garrick himself held.[25] Affairs rested thus until 1778 when Sheridan bought Lacy's moiety at a price of thirty-thousand guineas, plus a lifetime annuity of one-thousand pounds. He then sold his own former holding to Linley and Ford, raising each of their portions to a quarter of the whole, and established himself sole proprietor of the other half. Of course, Garrick yet held the huge mortgage of twenty-two-thousand pounds; and Sheridan owed other creditors at least twenty-thousand pounds, which he borrowed at more than five per cent, offering the theater itself as security. His cash investment for the whole transaction seems not to have exceeded one-thousand-three-hundred pounds.

By the original plan, Thomas Sheridan was to be manager of acting for the new administration; Richard, business manager; and Thomas Linley, the director of music. Thomas Sheridan declined, but Richard and his father-in-law proceeded confidently, certain that "it must be an *infernal* management indeed"[26] that could not clear at least seven-thousand pounds annually from the theater. Beginning their campaign on September 21, 1776, they opened with a production of *Twelfth Night* accompanied by *New Brooms*, a prelude written especially for the occasion by George Colman the elder. And, in support of the campaign, Sheridan began revising old plays, like William Congreve's *The Old Bachelor*, and reviving tested favorites, like Nicholas Rowe's *Jane Shore*. Sheridan endured with patience the testiness of his actresses, and he staged for them such splendid productions as *Selima and Azor*, a romantic extravaganza scored by Linley and designed by De Loutherbourg. Sheridan wrote a fine epilogue for the *Semiramis* of George Edward

Ayscough, a tragedy left over from Garrick days; and he produced an adaptation of Shakespeare's *The Tempest* featuring special music by Thomas Linley, Junior. In the winter of that first season he extensively revised Sir John Vanbrugh's *The Relapse*, staging it under the title *A Trip to Scarborough*. He introduced exciting new talent in the person of "Perdita" Robinson, and he reversed at last the financial disappointments of the season by producing *The School for Scandal* in May.

But Sheridan's industry did not last. Even by July, 1777, Garrick was lamenting the sure misfortune of "poor old Drury!"; and by March, 1778, everyone was "raving against Mr. Sheridan for his supineness."[27] During the 1777 - 78 season, he wrote nothing new for production, thereby fairly dooming the season to financial disaster; and, by September, 1778, his father had acceded to the management at the earnest request of the proprietors. Of course, the autocratic tyranny of Thomas Sheridan brought little stability to the theater. After only two years the management reverted to interim appointees — Richard himself (1780 - 81) and the actor Joseph Younger (1781 - 82) — then settled upon Thomas King, who resigned it six years later because he had not even "sufficient authority to command the cleaning of a coat, or adding, by way of decoration, a yard of copper lace; both which, it must be allowed, were often wanted."[28] Since King's successor, John Philip Kemble, enjoyed relatively more of Sheridan's confidence than the others, he enjoyed relatively more autonomy. But none of them was ever really his own man because the chief proprietor could not permit them to be so.

And Sheridan wrought havoc at every turn. The star performers generally got at least part of their salaries, but the staff workers — carpenters, painters, understrappers — often went for months without pay.[29] And Sheridan bled the treasury unconscionably, sometimes scrawling frantic distress calls to his treasurer: "Beg, borrow, or steal; let me have thirty pounds, and send them by return post. Fear nothing, be civil to all claimants. Shut up the office, and write to me directly." "Borrow and fear not. Put £60 in your pocket, and come to me directly."[30]

Between 1776 and 1790 receipts at Drury Lane exceeded disbursements by a paltry average of only one-thousand-one-hundred pounds per annum, a far cry from the seven-thousand pounds' annual profit Sheridan had anticipated at the outset. The 1777 - 78 season showed profits on the account books of only ten pounds;

1787 - 88 showed a staggering deficit of about one-thousand-six-hundred-sixteen pounds. And the construction of the new Drury Lane between 1791 and 1794, a move calculated to restore some solvency, just darkened the fiscal destiny of the enterprise. Hoping to pay for the new building and to retire current mortgage debts, the management had raised one-hundred-fifty-thousand pounds by subscription. But building costs so far exceeded all estimates that the property remained encumbered by a debt of seventy-thousand pounds, foredooming the new theater, which was suited for little other than fancy spectacle anyway, to perpetual financial crisis.[31]

Complications succeeding from the costs of construction led at last to a Chancery suit in 1802 in which creditors threatened to attach the box-office receipts at Drury Lane. Decrying Sheridan's fiscal slovenliness, they charged that eight-thousand pounds was yet owing in land rent for the theater ground and that, by piling encumbrance upon encumbrance, Sheridan had concealed the mismanagement of thousands of pounds. In an eloquent two hour defense, he argued in turn that performers' salaries held first claims upon receipts. And, although he won his point, the Chancellor, who sharply rebuked him, cited Dr. Johnson's maxim "that negligence and irregularity long continued will make knowledge useless, wit ridiculous, and genius contemptible."[32]

Of course, Sheridan's "negligence and irregularity" did not limit themselves to fiscal matters. Manuscripts submitted for consideration remained forever unread; solicitations from authors, though politely received, languished unconcluded. Indeed, so casual and vulnerable was the management that it even fell victim to an outrageous hoaxer, William Ireland, who in 1796 persuaded Sheridan that a tragedy called *Vortigern and Rowena* (really Ireland's own forgery) was a lost play by Shakespeare. The Drury Lane company produced the play handsomely, with John Philip Kemble as Vortigern, but it was hooted off the stage in the third act.

In his important contribution to *The London Stage*, Charles Beecher Hogan demonstrates that during the Sheridan years Drury Lane was relatively less innovative than Covent Garden. Under the management of Thomas Harris, Covent Garden brought out one hundred nineteen new mainpieces between 1776 and 1800 as opposed to ninety at Drury Lane; and two-hundred-forty-seven new afterpieces as opposed to one-hundred-thirty-five. The difference relates mainly, says Mr. Hogan, to Harris's steadier enterprise and daring — to his ability to wheedle from reliable authors the work they had in hand by promising them liberal fees and good productions.[33] Sheridan's partiality for his own plays, together with his notorious neglect of the manuscripts submitted to him, certainly also discouraged new material at Drury Lane — as did Kemble's preference for tested stock pieces, plays by Shakespeare, John Fletcher, Thomas Otway, William Congreve, Colley Cibber, George Farquhar, etc. Furthermore, Drury Lane was a company of great actors, especially tragic actors; and, since comic compositions outnumbered tragic ones by at least five to one, according to Mr. Hogan, fewer new plays immediately fitted the acting specialties of the Drury Lane company.[34]

But, despite its more conservative repertory, it performed during the Sheridan years as varied a program as Covent Garden; both theaters averaged fifty different mainpieces a season and forty different afterpieces. It also enjoyed a respectable number of special successes, such as James Cobb's two comic operas *The Haunted Tower,* which ran fifty-six nights in the 1789 - 90 season, and *The Siege of Belgrade,* which ran forty-four nights in 1790 - 91. In 1797 - 98, M. G. Lewis's *The Castle-Spectre* ran for forty-seven nights. The immensely popular boy prodigy William Henry West Betty performed quite profitably in 1804. And, of course, Sheridan scored his own special record of success with *The Critic, The Stranger, Pizarro,* and certainly *The School for Scandal,* which had two-hundred-sixty-one performances by the end of 1800.[35] In fact, the account books show, especially after 1790, that Drury Lane would have surpassed the earnings of its sister theater had it not been so encumbered by gigantic debts.[36]

On February 24, 1809, Drury Lane burned to the ground. Although valued at a quarter of a million pounds, it was insured for only thirty-five thousand; and nothing was saved from the flames but an iron chest containing the patent and other legal documents. Financially ruined, but as resilient as always, Sheridan immediately set out to rebuild; he first established the company at the Lyceum Theatre, then called upon Samuel Whitbread, a successful brewer and a colleague in Parliament, to form a committee to establish solvency and plan reconstruction. Whitbread willingly undertook the task, but he firmly stipulated that Sheridan should have "no concern or connexion of any kind whatever with the new undertaking."[37] Only on these terms would anyone consider joining the committee, and Whitbread enforced them absolutely.

In settling the debts accumulated against the theater — debts running to over four-hundred-thousand pounds — the committee assessed Sheridan's half-ownership at twenty-four-thousand pounds and his interests in the fruit offices and private boxes at four-thousand pounds.[38] At his own suggestion, payment of his claim was reserved until after the theater should be built. He also empowered the committee to appropriate from his claim the money owing to his creditors, an amount probably exceeding the claim itself. And thus he linked the ends of his theatrical and Parliamentary careers. For, in seeking re-election for Stafford in 1812, he found no money available to him; and, in the shock of defeat, he rebuked Whitbread passionately: "On the subject of your refusing to advance to me the £ 2,000 I applied for to take with me to Stafford out of the large sum confessedly due to me (unless I signed some paper containing I know not what — and which you presented to my breast like a cocked pistol on the last day I saw you) I will not dwell. *This and this alone lost me my election.*"[39]

III *Parliamentarian*

The career thus so wretchedly ended had begun quite auspiciously in October, 1780, when Sheridan had entered the House of Commons to represent Stafford. Charles James Fox and the Whig establishment at Devonshire House had supported his candidacy, and he had won election as running mate with Colonel Edward Monckton. Sheridan's fragmentary essays of the Waltham Abbey period clearly attest his early ambitions for a political career. And, even after earning fame as a dramatist, he nurtured this ambition by writing for *The Englishman,* a periodical published between March 13 and June 2, 1779, to attack Lord North's administration.[40] Early in 1780, before entering Parliament, Sheridan served as sub-chairman of the Westminster Association for Reform, urging universal suffrage and annual Parliaments, and in the cause of the association he worked closely with Charles James Fox, whose zeal for Parliamentary reform attracted Sheridan to the Whig party. The friendship with Fox at first gave great promise; but, even during the 1780's, fissures began showing in it because of disagreements over the Gaming Laws and the Marriage Act and the jealousies aggravated by the first Regency Crisis in 1788. Consequently, Sheridan failed to receive a cabinet post, one actually promised him, when Fox took office with "All the Talents" in 1806.

But, while great power largely eluded Sheridan, his long political career saw moments of high honor and major responsibility. On November 2, 1780, for example, while yet basking in Fox's favor, he was elected to Brooks's Club, the gaming center of the Foxites. Sixteen months later, during the brief ministry of Lord Rockingham (March to July, 1782), he took office as Under-Secretary of State and declined cabinet rank for want of experience. In April, 1783, he entered the coalition government of Fox and Lord North as Secretary to the Treasury; and, had the Regency succeeded in 1788 - 89, transferring to the Prince of Wales the authority of the crown during the King's mental illness, he would most likely have served as Treasurer to the Navy, the post he at last took during "All the Talents" in 1806 when he was denied the cabinet position he expected and deserved. Throughout most of his career, of course, he served with the opposition; and in this service he won heroic distinction as a prosecutor in the impeachment of Warren Hastings, 1787 - 88, and as a voice of reason after the mutinies at Spithead and the Nore, in 1797, when his call for Parliamentary unity enabled the government to deal firmly with the mutineers.

But, whether in office or out, Sheridan continued something of a radical. He doggedly championed freedom of the press, abolition of slavery, and Catholic emancipation. He defended Home Rule, challenged English coercion of the Irish Parliament, and hailed the French Revolution as a glorious blow for freedom, a stroke against tyranny (and thereby sacrificed his friendship with Edmund Burke). He deplored the English policy of war with revolutionary France, even while demanding staunch resistance to Napoleon Bonaparte. He urged Parliamentary reform, pressed reform in the Penal Laws, damned the Corn Laws, and called for moderation of the Alien's Bill. Except for his defense of the theatrical monopoly, which to him was more a personal economic concern than a political one, he rejoiced in liberal causes, and he proclaimed his causes eagerly.[41]

In proclaiming them, he wrote political pamphlets on such matters as Indian affairs and absentee landlords from Ireland.[42] But, more importantly, he managed the daily press for his party; and he matched wits with his conservative opposite, George Rose, to control at all times the editorial policy of at least one London newspaper. According to Lucyle Werkmeister, who has studied the daily press of the period, he more than once influenced every single newspaper in London to the side of the opposition; and he was not above having Drury Lane Theatre thought the voice of English Liberalism, where plays might exude Liberal innuendo and actors supply political comment extempore.[43]

But, of course, the main expression of his conviction was in

Parliamentary speech; and he spoke on virtually every major issue of his age. His maiden speech, given only a month after he entered the House, proved somewhat disappointing. It answered a charge of fraud brought against his own election in Staffordshire and perforce adjusted itself to a low and earnest key.[44] Perhaps it also suffered from the "thick and indistinct mode of delivery" said by Moore to characterize his early speeches.[45] But, whatever the problem, he corrected it quickly, bending the resources of his arresting eyes, his commanding presence, and glittering wit to the indomitable drive of his principles.

Early in his career, he prepared his speeches quite carefully; and, while he quickly enough lost patience with research, he always showed astonishing facility for extemporaneous presentation. Allowing himself only a few moments' briefing, he then organized and amplified his subject as he talked from rough notes. He displayed immense talent for witty analogies, precise hypotheses, and an easy flair for delightful quips and rejoinders; but, to reinforce the much-admired spontaneity of his wit, he stocked his commonplace book with sportive thoughts and dazzling phrases. He could disarm antagonism by bringing the House into good humor, but he more often joined attack by sifting out the flaws in an opposing view and thus challenging the competence of his adversary, whose inconsistency, arrogance, corruption, ignorance, and falsehood he scrupulously detailed. Generally avoiding brutal invective, he chose instead to dissect his opponent with a sharp-edged wit; and he especially liked to re-interpret the words of the opposing argument and to make them favor his own side of the issue, which he subtly represented as ethically secure and as closely attuned to his own sincerity, consistency, geniality, selflessness, and keen good sense.[46]

His best speech is thought to be the first one he delivered against Warren Hastings. It began at 6:30 on the evening of February 7, 1787; and, when it ended five hours later, it brought "the whole House, the members, peers, and strangers involuntarily" to "a tumult of applause."[47] Even William Pitt conceded that an abler speech had never been made, and Fox declared it unequivocally the best speech ever given within the walls of Parliament. But, because it was badly reported, its real excellence is now quite lost. Much more accurately reported is the second of his speeches against Hastings, the one delivered at Westminster Hall over a period of four days, June 3, 6, 10, 13, in 1788. This second speech, like the first one, argued the third charge in the impeachment of Hastings: the responsibility he bore in sacking the treasuries of the Begums of Oude, two princesses whose son and grandson, the Vizier of Oude, owed money to the East India Company, of which Hastings was Governor General between 1773 and 1785. Sheridan delivered the speech before packed galleries, many of whom had paid fifty pounds for a ticket; and he again won effusive praise. Burke called the speech "the most astonishing effort of eloquence, argument and wit united, of which there is any record or tradition."[48]

As a comment on evidence against Hastings, the Westminster Hall speech follows a logical linear form, systematically discrediting the arguments for the defense, systematically affirming the evidence for the prosecution. But the presiding unity of the speech turns upon Sheridan's imaginative rendering of the abstract issue, the conflict between charity and deliberate tyranny. The chief agent for charity is of course God himself whose influence delivers evidence to the prosecution and supports its cause. Allied with God are patriotic fervor, filial piety, maternal and magisterial sanctity, concern for the weak, protection of the innocent, and certainly justice, the "abstract idea of all that would be perfect in the spirits and aspirings of men!"[49]

As agent for deliberate tyranny, Hastings emerges in the speech as a "monster in nature" whose crimes issue not from passion (as did those of Nero and Caligula) but from cool and rational deliberation. In characterizing this protean monster, Sheridan labels him an apostate to humanity, a prince of darkness gifted at causing vice to masquerade as virtue. In the sense that "consummate craft" reflects prudence, says Sheridan, Hastings has sought to effect the coexistence of prudence and vice, a union generally thought impossible, and has turned the devices of truth to the ends of treachery. "But my Lords," Sheridan urgently asks, "do you, the judges of this land . . . do you approve of this mockery, and call it the character of justice, which takes the *form of right* to excite wrong?"[50]

In resolving the abstract issues of the case, Sheridan unmasks the pretenses of tyranny, explodes the masquerade of false justice, and elevates true justice to the enlightened view, "where the mind rises; where the heart expands; where the countenance is ever placid and benign; where her favorite attitude is to stoop to the unfortunate; to hear their cry and to help them."[51] Amplifying the logical examination of the evidence, then, is a sustained structural metaphor, a figurative war between heaven and hell in which subtle intellectual evil threatens the dominion of God and Charity.

On seeing Hastings at Brighton Pavilion in 1805, Sheridan insisted that he had intended no personal malice in his speech. And, given the figurative strategies of the speech, this disclaimer need not seem insincere. For, like the Begums on their side, Hastings had served to embody one element of a large moral conflict; and, in pursuing the implications of the crimes alleged, Sheridan had shaped Hastings into a symbol of unthinkable treachery, directing his contempt more vehemently against the symbol than the man.

The Westminster Hall speech marked the zenith of Sheridan's political career, a career showing flashes of glory but really enjoying no comfortable stability. Michael Sadler attributes this instability chiefly to Sheridan's long friendship with the Prince of Wales, a friendship which aggravated the jealousies and hostilities of Sheridan's colleagues. Sheridan eventually suffered from the faithlessness of the Prince himself, whose petulance during the Second Regency Crisis in 1811 not only contravened Sheridan's counsel but also shattered his political hopes.[52] After the death of Fox in 1806, Sheridan had stood for Westminster, seeking the prestige of Fox's seat, and had won narrowly. On standing again for Westminster in 1807, he lost quite decisively but was returned for Ilchester, a borough held at the Prince's disposal. To escape all political obligation to the Prince, Sheridan sought his old seat for Stafford in 1812 but was unsuccessful.

With the loss of Parliamentary immunities, he suffered every indignity his creditors could heap upon him, even enduring three nights in the spunging house in August, 1813. But, by 1813, he was certainly no stranger to distress: he had lost Eliza in 1792; an infant daughter had died four months later; and his son Tom, a consumptive, continued a source of limitless racking concern to him. Moreover, Sheridan's second marriage, to Hester Ogle in 1795, brought him only nominal happiness, though it did bring him a second son, Charles Brinsley, and of course the Drury Lane fire had cost him everything. But even the darkest distresses of his life could not really stifle his "most unfortunately sanguine temper," nor could the ignominy of debts and duns really supplant his immense popularity. When he died on July 7, 1816, his grateful countrymen buried him in the Poets' Corner. Certainly no one buried there could have built a more erratic literary record; but Sheridan merited recognition not merely for the great comedies everyone knew but also for the ideas and experiments tucked away in jottings and juvenilia and in a great variety of little-known, perhaps then even unknown, efforts. From such places Sheridan emerges now a comprehensive and versatile, if uneven and sporadic, literary thinker and doer — not just as a playwright, certainly, but also as a poet of some force and diversity and as a literary theorist of some daring and perception.

CHAPTER 2

Literary Theorist

T HE fragment on prosody written soon after Sheridan left
Harrow (1768 or '69) seems to mark his first significant
venture into literary theory. Apparently intended as an answer to
John Foster's "Essay on Accent and Quantity" (1762), it argues that
metrical rules should be reduced from musical harmony. "Every Nation finds out for itself a natural melody," the young theorist affirms;
the ancient Greeks had their melodies; the English now have theirs.
And, since modern Englishmen have no idea how ancient Greek
melodies sounded, it is futile for modern critics to judge the melody
of English verse by ancient rules. There is a bit more to the argument, the idea that "our verse depends on *time* and *quantity* only,"
that "we may vary the accent as we please and the propriety is in doing so melodiously," that "A verse should read itself into harmony,
else if it depend only on the chant of the Reader there is no such
thing as actual rithm."[1]

But Sheridan's jottings break off before they are marshaled into
any really articulate discourse,[2] and he apparently never again
attempted a prose treatise on poetic theory. In two satiric poems,
however — one written in 1771; the other probably in 1774 — he
amplified his poetic manifesto by commenting indirectly on metrics,
diction, and decorum, and by suggesting the relative artistic merit of
several poetic types. Apart from the fragment against Sir William
Temple and some brief comments in the letters to Grenville, comments duplicated in his fragmentary treatise on female education
(a piece discussed later in Chapter 4), he seems to have said
nothing about prose or fiction. But the preface to his translation
from Aristaenetus offers yet other views on poetry; and from
his prologues and epilogues and from his burlesque play *The
Critic* some idea of his views on drama and dramaturgy can be
obtained.

I   *"Clio's Protest"* and *"A Familiar Epistle"*: *Poetry and the Poet*

The first of his satiric essays in criticism, "Clio's Protest, or the
Picture Varnish'd," young Sheridan wrote in reply to a wretched
doggerel piece called "The Bath Picture," a spineless panegyric on
women of social prominence in Bath. Wholly innocent of energy and
ingenuity, "The Picture" whines feebly through twenty or so bland
quatrains, asserting no clarity in imagery or logic, reflecting no taste
or judgment. Signed "Pindar," a pseudonym for Miles Peter An-
drews, it claims the heavenly inspiration of the muse Clio — and
Sheridan's answer sharply vindicates the outraged muse.

At the outset of his four-part argument, he declares himself legal
advocate for Clio and affirms by an affidavit sworn before Jupiter
that the muse in no way inspired "The Bath Picture." Very likely, he
suggests, dullness had done the inspiring. Next, he offers logical
evidence to support the affidavit — that Clio certainly knew how to
spell and to point periods, as Pindar apparently did not, and that, as
sister to Apollo, she probably knew a great deal about rhyme and
meter, as Pindar clearly did not. Then follows, in the long middle
section of the poem, a close, virtually line-by-line, review of "The
Picture" which satirically specifies its failings and suggests ways to
improve it. The argument concludes by advising Pindar to cease
murdering people with insipid panegyric and to take up satire,
which in his hands would do less damage than panegyric.

As the poem speeds along on brisk octasyllabic couplets, the
speaker sometimes shares critical confidences with his reader,
sometimes directly chides or corrects the inept Pindar. A light,
goliardic spirit commands the piece, but young Sheridan makes absolutely clear his serious distaste for Pindar's artistic shabbiness,
criticizing "The Picture" against his own clearly perceptible poetic
principles. In damning Pindar's halting meters, for example,
Sheridan certainly evokes the theory of poetic time suggested in his
answer to Dr. Foster. In fact, he here places the theory in an apt
musical context, advising the lovely Miss Calder — one of the vic-
tims of Pindar's panegyric — to pay "more regard to *time*"[3] in her
dancing than Pindar had done in his versifying. Later in the poem,
Sheridan's embryonic answer to Dr. Foster is again hinted at in the
hypothesis that, should Pindar become "*Laureate* in the Skies," his
verse — utterly impoverished of melodious accent and metrical harmony — would ultimately "spoil the *music* of the spheres" (115). As
a comprehensive critical comment, of course, "Clio's Protest" goes

far beyond the unfinished little prose treatise; and its judgments, stated as broad poetic principles, might be set forth as follows:

Language. Good poetry must utilize the conventional word stock. Poets, therefore, have no license to coin new terms, to distort conventional syntax, to violate accepted grammatical canons, or to indulge linguistic affectations, such as altering parts of speech for poetic effect. Certainly no poet may depart from customary usage merely to meet the exigencies of rhyme or meter (108, 110).

Rhymè, Meter, and *Harmony.* Rhyme in good poetry should show a certain freshness and ingenuity. If rhyming terms merely satisfy the reader's expectations, they minimize, rather than enrich, poetic effectiveness (109, 116). Furthermore, the "bonds of metre" (108) ought always to control the accentual rhetoric of the poem. They should not be broken asunder by such other conceptual demands as phrasing or wit (108, 109) but should complement these demands, contributing with them to a harmony of verse and theme (115).

Decorum and *Invention.* Scrupulous decorum should govern poetic use of personified abstractions. "Envy," for example, should not be pictured as "looking pleasant" (109). Furthermore, the poet's inventive faculty should anticipate and control the associations evoked by allusions and metaphors. Invention should also properly encompass the poetic subject. In other words, Fancy should, as Sheridan puts it, "display its wit" (116) to exploit as fully as possible the thematic, descriptive, and allusive potential of the subject treated (111, 114, 116).

The Canons of Common Sense. The final test of poetic effectiveness is common sense, and poets are well advised to apply this test to their art and to forgo vain appeals to the Muses (118). In short, good poetry represents not fevered inspiration but careful work — to forge the meter and select the rhymes, to harmonize theme and form. "You write with *ease,* to show your breeding," says Sheridan to poor Pindar. "But *easy writing's* vile *hard reading*" (117).

The second of young Sheridan's satiric essays in criticism, "A Familiar Epistle to the Author of the Heroic Epistle to Sir William Chambers," curiously turns political satire to literary-critical objectives.[4] In attacking party bigotry, it systematically damns the literary failings of the "Heroic Postscript," a poem claiming for its author, William Mason, major credit for promoting important naval reforms. According to Mason, who signs himself "Sancho," these reforms resulted from the publication of his earlier verse satire, a "Heroic

Epistle." In Sheridan's "Familiar Epistle," the progress of the argument clearly recalls "Clio's Protest." After the prologue generally condemns Sancho's literary offenses, a close "review" of the "Heroic Postscript" indicates its specific failings and recommends corrective action. Finally comes the admonition that Sancho, if he must write, find himself a new mode of writing. As Pindar had been advised to swap panegyric for satire, so Sancho is urged to exchange satire for lyric — literary hate for literary love. Furthermore, the catalogue of Sancho's artistic lacunae recalls the sorts of poetic failings damned in "Clio's Protest": feeble rhymes, faltering metrics, confused tropes, bad grammar, false concord, logical gaps, departures from common sense, especially in grammatical logic and in the government of personifications (181; 194 - 95).[5]

"A Familiar Epistle," however, goes much beyond the earlier poem in commenting upon the forms and functions of poetry. It insists throughout, for example, that satire makes for inferior art, especially satire attacking specific political adversaries, rather than mankind generally (177, 185, 186). Moreover, satire lacks permanence because it magnifies the ugliness of nature and so departs from the proper province of poetic art (179). According to Sheridan, the good poet properly plays his fancy throughout all nature's wide domain, seeking to discover her beauties and to give them luster through art. Art, therefore, intensifies the creativity of natural creation. If, however, the ranging fancy recognizes in natural creation weaknesses not subject to artistic correction, it properly conceals them, rather than exposing and heightening them through satire.

Poetry of the highest order appears, then, in the "chaste and moral lay" of such "mildly melancholy" poets as Thomas Gray, or in the buccolics of William Shenstone, or in the sad love elegies of James Hammond (186). These kinds of poems, Sheridan suggests, betoken a fancy keyed to the beneficent impulses of the heart. They make no appeal to heated passion. To reason, they are forever just and logical. In application, they are universal and timeless (186; 178 - 79).

II *Further Reflections on Poetry:* The Love Epistles of Aristaenetus

Complementing and extending the poetic principles suggested in "Clio's Protest" and in "A Familiar Epistle" are additional reflections on poetry in the preface and notes to *The Love Epistles of Aristaenetus,* the verse translation published by Sheridan and his friend Nathaniel Brassey Halhed in August, 1771. In their prefatory comment, the translators freely admit that, *"pleasing as they are,"* the epistles *"have scarcely anything original in them, being a cento from the writing of Plato, Lucian, Philostratus, and almost all the ancient Greek authors."*[6] Although seeing the epistles as *"terse, elegant, and very poetical, both in language, and sentiment,"* the translators admit that Aristaenetus is *"an undistinguished and almost unknown ancient."*[7] In short, they admit to "Englishing" an obscure and inferior Greek poetaster. Consequently, their preface — signed with the combined initials "H. S." but chiefly written by Sheridan, as Halhed attests[8] — assumes importance first of all as a curious critical apologia and as an interesting eighteenth-century philosophy of translation.

As a critical apologia, it justifies, on grounds serviceable to an appreciation of T. S. Eliot's early poetry, the poem pieced together as an allusive mosaic. Such a poem *"opens to us a new source of entertainment"* both by inviting consideration of the poet's taste in selecting allusions and by exciting admiration of his talents in applying them. Furthermore, the new poem derives dignity and thematic substance from the authority and artistic merit of the original works, *"the works from whence these sweets are extracted."* To say, then, that a poem is a patchwork of borrowed phrases is not therefore to *"depreciate the performance,"* assuming the borrowed phrases are artistically interwoven.[9]

In commenting upon translation, the preface to *The Love Epistles of Aristaenetus* affirms a highly liberal philosophy that suggests, at its extremest point, that the text translated need only supply the subject of an otherwise completely new piece of literature. After studying the theory of translation in the eighteenth century, J. W. Draper concludes that the century "inherited a tradition of free translations, of translations, not for their own sake, but for the enrichment of the vernacular." To this tradition it added "a more strictly moral aim, the cultivation of good manners, of propriety and decorum; and it proceeded to cut, to refine, and to embellish, along these lines."[10] Throughout the century, writes Draper, expurgation was expected of translators. Force of expression properly prevailed over fidelity. In full accord, therefore, with presiding conventions, Halhed and Sheridan freely excise all indecencies (or so they say). They happily translate Greek prose into English poetry, explaining that English prose fails to capture the poetic quality of the original. And they comfortably announce that *"where the subject would admit of it"* they have developed new ideas for the text, a license mollified, they suggest, by a style closely redolent of the original — the style Aristaenetus would have used had these *"new ideas"* been his. It is hardly surprising, then, to find the translators openly declaring at last that they have signed Aristaenetus' name to several altogether new poems, with thanks to him only for the poetic subjects used.

The liberal philosophy of translation espoused by the two young poets easily embraces the leading artistic aims of their work: (1) to introduce into the English language a species of poetry called *simplex munditiis,* a poetic mode characterized by thoughts *"spirited and fanciful,"* a style *"simple, yet not inelegant"*[11] and (2) to demonstrate in poetic art an apt interrelationship between theme and form. Rooted in Horace (Ode V; Book I) and finding expression in the seventeenth-century lyricism of Ben Jonson and Robert Herrick,[12] the doctrine of *simplex munditiis* specifically defines "simple elegance" in feminine cosmetic and dress. In *Tatler 151,* for example, Steele holds that "nothing touches our imagination so much as a beautiful woman in a plain dress." In eighteenth-century England, however, so handy a doctrine could hardly escape application to other concepts of simplicity — simple elegance in manner, in taste, in literary style. As R. D. Havens suggests, Addison's view that "those only who are endowed with a true Greatness of Soul and Genius can . . . admire Nature in her Simplicity and Nakedness" encourages a general association of simplicity and elegance;[13] and such an association certainly colors the literary thought of Swift, Goldsmith, David Hume, Joshua Reynolds, and William Cowper — to say nothing of the two young "translators" of Aristaenetus.

As apparently understood by Halhed and Sheridan, the doctrine of *simplex munditiis* combats the principle of "a special diction for poetry," a principle widely current during the closing decades of the century, especially among periodical reviewers.[14] In urging in their preface that poetry seek to *"redeem our language from the imputation of barbarity,"*[15] they join Goldsmith's assault against those misguided poetic innovators who have resolved the language into a "pristine barbarity" by indulging themselves "in the most licentious transpositions, and the harshest constructions, vainly imagining that the more their writings are unlike prose, the more they resemble poetry."[16] The two young poets see the doctrine of *simplex munditiis* to be the proper alternative to these barbarities; and the major implications of this doctrine apparently accord with William Cowper's appeal for a poetry intended "to make verse speak the language of prose without being prosaic, to marshal the words of it in such an order as they might naturally take in falling from the lips of an extemporary speaker, yet without meanness, harmoniously, elegantly and without seeming to displace a syllable for the sake of rhyme."[17]

Consequently, Halhed and Sheridan congratulate themselves for rendering Aristaenetus into a plain but elegant English, an English free of extravagant "poetic" conventions and drawn from the vocabulary of polite conversation. Here is an instance from the first epistle as translated by Sheridan:

> Her lips of deeper red, how thin!
> How nicely white the teeth within
> Her nose how taper to the tip
> And slender as her ruby lip!

The description runs on in this vein for twenty or so lines (certainly simple if not wholly elegant), and of the entire portrait the translators remark: "This description differs in one circumstance from the usual poetic analysis of beauty, which is this, that (if we except the epithets 'ruby,' 'snowy,' &c., which could not well have been avoided) the lady it paints would be really beautiful; whereas it is generally said, 'that a negro would be handsome compared to a woman in poetical dress.' "[18] Later they applaud the images of Epistle III as being "extremely natural and simple, though the expression is glowing and luxurious."[19] In both these glosses, they reflect the *simplex munditiis* doctrine. To be sure, their efforts at "simple elegance" are not uniformly successful, and in their preface they admit as much. But by attempting the practice, and by pointing its artistic merit, they place their little book among the immediate literary antecedents to Wordsworth's important theories of poetic diction.

The second of the major artistic aims governing the translation — that demonstrating in poetic art an apt interrelationship between theme and form — finds Sheridan urging theories of unity strongly argued by his father and also advocated in his own "Clio's Protest." In 1762, in *A Course of Lectures on Elocution*, Thomas Sheridan had roundly damned all poets who failed to adapt their prosody to their subject matter. Such puerile composition, he charged, produces a metrical uniformity altogether "insupportable to the ear," one which necessarily "wearies attention."[20] The preface to Aristaenetus picks up this strain en route to "Clio's Protest," justifying through it the metrical varieties of the epistles translated: "*in general, the par-*

*ticular strain of each Epistle suggested the particular measure in
which it is written. Had they been all in one kind of verse, they
would have fatigued, they might have disgusted. At present, it is
hoped that some analogy will be found between the mode of passion
in each Epistle, and the versification by which it is expressed.*"[21]

III   Sheridan's Poetic Theory and the Critical Tradition

As reflected in these four early works — "Clio's Protest," "A
Familiar Epistle," the translations from Aristaenetus, and the
fragmentary treatise on prosody — Sheridan's poetic theory typifies
eighteenth-century English criticism in transition. Basically, it is
rationalistic. Like Samuel Johnson and Lord Kames, for example,
Sheridan rejects neo-Classical rules and purports to measure artistic
merit by impartial logical tests.[22] Like the typical rationalist critic,
furthermore, he identifies reason as the foundation for taste[23] and
considers common sense the final arbiter of artistic durability.[24] Certainly the rationalist view governs his concept of "correctness" —
though his obsession with grammatical and dictional propriety more
closely recalls the criticism of George Lowth, the grammarian, than
that of Dr. Johnson[25] — and very likely rationalism promotes his distaste for empty rhymes; for here he attests, at least by implication,
that the pleasures of rhyme engage a rational awareness of the
meanings of words, not just a sensational response to their sounds.[26]
Comparably, his defense of the poem as an allusive mosaic seems
rooted in rationalist concepts of allusion — in the tacit assumption
that readers will recognize and interpret echoes of other poems
(though in justifying frequent allusion to *contemporary* poetry he
takes something of a new departure). And his theory of verse translation essentially falls into the rationalist camp, recalling Dryden's
famous definitions of "paraphrase" and "imitation" in his preface to
Ovid's Epistles.

Though rarely venturing beyond sight of his rationalism, Sheridan
hazards a few cautious sallies into other eighteenth-century critical
domains. His concept of artistic imitation, for example, holds quite
rationalistically that poetic imagination properly seeks to improve
Nature;[27] but a further suggestion — that for improving Nature (for
aspiring to an ideal Nature) poetry deserves the name "divine" —
finds him courting a neo-Platonic doctrine widely espoused
throughout the century.[28] Similarly, his mistrust of satire reflects a
neat critical dualism, at once reflecting the rationalist view that
satire lacks universality (and therefore permanence) because of its

particularity,[29] and the imaginationist view that satire is transitory because it eschews beneficent passions.[30] Much the same sort of dualism sees him affirming, on the one hand, that poetry emerges from hard work fathered by common sense, while he suggests, on the other, that the creative Fancy finds significant stimulus in passionate sympathies.[31] In insisting, furthermore, that personified abstractions not disappoint conventional expectation, he accords with rationalistic theories of poetic generality. His taste for concrete description, however, finds him steering a middle course between the conservative rationalist, who denounces the particularizing effects of graphic detail, and the liberal imaginationist, who encourages close description. Steering his middle way, he insists upon a graphic particularity at least sufficient to control the reader's visual associations.[32]

Certainly Sheridan's prosody represents his most daring venture into relatively uncharted critical reaches. Both by correlating the canons of music and verse and by urging accentual concepts of metrical analysis, he anticipates significant tenets of Romantic prosody. Professor Paul Fussell indicates, in studying the *Theory of Prosody in Eighteenth-Century England*,[33] that syllabism dominated the first forty years of the century. Springing from French origins, promoted by neo-Classical concepts of order (both moral and artistic), and perpetuated by Edward Bysshe's influential *The Art of English Poetry* (1702), the syllabist doctrine insisted upon strictly regularized patterns of syllabic stress in English poetry.[34] Even after 1770 this conservative doctrine largely obtained in the criticism of such giants as Johnson and Kames, though for two decades imaginative prosodists, John Brown and Daniel Webb among them,[35] had urged more liberal views. In saying, therefore — as Sheridan does in his fragmentary answer to Dr. Foster — that "we may vary accent as we please and the propriety is in doing so melodiously," young Sheridan flies violently in the face of ordered rationalist prosody. With his father, with Webb, with Brown, with Richard Hurd, and with a few other mid-century theorists, he states the case for the liberal accentualist.[36]

In basing prosody upon musical analogies, Sheridan further aligns himself with a select group of daring contemporary theorists.[37] According to J. W. Draper, in a discussion of poetry and music in eighteenth-century aesthetics, neo-Classical criticism had evidenced "but little knowledge of music in either the abstract or the concrete."[38] Not only did critics find the musical esthetic confusing and difficult; they also felt musical appeal to be largely emotional and therefore dangerous to the proper intellectual interests of art. Continuing speculation on the psychology of artistic response, however, finally pointed up the tonal and rhythmic similarities of music and poetry and gave rise, according to Draper's account, to some thirty treatises on the subject between 1750 and 1770.[39] Several of these pieces advance the equal-time theory of metrical scansion, an accentualist concept touched on in Sheridan's unfinished essay.[40] And at least one of them suggests, as he does, that since melodic properties vary from language to language, no single set of prosodic rules can serve the analysis of all poetries.[41]

By far the more significant of these concepts, of course, is the equal-time theory, which equates the poetic foot to the musical bar, thus allowing a variety of syllabic patterns within a given unit of metrical time. In supporting the argument that "our verse depends on *time* and *quantity* only" (to use Sheridan's phrase), this theory utterly denies the syllabist doctrine and anticipates in important ways the metrical conventions of Romantic poetry.[42] It places Sheridan at the farthest remove from his basic critical rationalism; and, with the *simplex mundittis* concept of poetic diction, it points decisively toward the presiding poetic theory of the later century.

IV   The Prologues and Epilogues: Tragedy, Comedy, Sentimental Comedy

As a theorist of drama, Sheridan again looks before and after; he embraces quite conventional theories of tragedy but offers to revise contemporary tastes for comedy. With Garrick and Goldsmith, he joins vigorous battle against sentimental (or "genteel") comedy and promotes instead what historians of drama often call "laughing comedy," comedy gathering principles from Classical and native antecedents — purposing to expose the follies of the lower and middle ranks of society — but recognizing that laughter as a judgmental phenomenon need not be cruel and derisive. Like sentimental comedy, "laughing comedy" accepts and encourages basic good nature in man; but it acknowledges lapses in human benevolence and distils merriment (more often amiable than derisive) from them. What Sheridan had to say about this comedy — and about tragedy and sentimental comedy — he said in several of the twelve prologues and epilogues he wrote between 1775 and 1781.

In 1776, for example, his epilogue to Captain Ayscough's

Semiramis admonishes the audience to "Go — and on *real* misery bestow/ The bless'd effusion of fictitious woe!" (272).[43] Behind this admonition to pious action rests the commonplace that tragedy properly inspires pity; and, by testimony of this same epilogue, pity is held to be a pleasurable emotion. A high and laudable emotion, it is capable of enlivening and enriching the soul and, at the same time, of motivating people to virtuous deeds. Since the pity generated by tragedy transcends rational judgment, good tragedy should be judged not by the critical mind but by the "feeling heart."[44] If the "Fancy'd grief" generated by tragedy succeeds in promoting actual piety, tragic art then merits the title "divine." To Sheridan, apparently, the highest manifestations of tragic art successfully translate pity from the fictive dramatic situation to the actual woes of actual men.

It is not surprising, then, that the prologue to *Sir Thomas Overbury* (1777) favors domestic tragedy over Classical tragedy. The premise developed appears as early as 1703 in Nicholas Rowe's prologue to *The Fair Penitent*,[45] and it receives even more famous treatment in George Lillo's preface to *The London Merchant* (1731). It holds that the woes of great Classical heroes have no intense and lasting effect upon the pity of the audience; instead, Classical tragedy inspires respect for the noble sufferer rather than pity for him. Since reason tells the playgoer that he can never himself experience the sorrows of great men, he cannot be deeply piteous of these sorrows and can therefore experience no motivation for continuining benevolence through them. Everyone, however, can identify his own conscience with the throes of "private guilt"; and everyone can experience in his own heart the dramatic conflicts (among private men) between high honor and base passion. Dramatic representation of domestic woes, then, best generates the enduring and practical pity necessary to the highest forms of tragic art.

Both the prologue to *Sir Thomas Overbury* and the tenth-night prologue to *The Rivals* emphasize guilt as the mainspring of tragedy. Apparently, tragic action properly dramatizes the triumph of virtue over guilt and, in the process, provokes pity for suffering innocence. To experience this pity is to embrace virtue and to discern moral truth. It is worth noting that Sheridan nowhere mentions "catharsis" or "fear." He is Aristotelian only in the sense that his references to "guilt" might imply some form of Classical "hamartia." Quite consistently, his prologues and epilogues champion tragedy of pathos, after the traditions of Otway and Rowe and after the prevailing tastes of his day.[46]

Sheridan's chief comments on comedy appear in the tenth-night prologue to *The Rivals*, where Mrs. Bulkley points to the figure of comedy and delineates the character in its face. In this face one should see, she says, "Humour quaint and sly," dimpling the cheek and brightening the eye. Also radiating from the face is "gay Invention" boasting its wiles "In amorous hint, and half-triumphant smiles."[47] In lines not easy to interpret, the prologue suggests that the best comedy dulls the sharp edge of satire, that it provokes through wit an awareness of human foibles, but that it avoids fierce corrective cruelties. Direct preachment, in any case, lies outside its province. Comic trickery cannot ably serve moral truth; light comic scenes can add no strength to "Holy laws."[48] In sum, the proper spirit of comedy is mirth and youthful vitality; the proper subject of comedy is love; the proper source of comedy is the cleverly imagined comic situation. In emphasizing the quaintness and slyness of humor and in pointing out the amorous hint and half-triumphant smiles of comic invention, Sheridan implies that a light irony inheres in the well-drawn comic situation. Comedy delights in playing jokes on people; it delights in inviting their confidence with one or another sort of "amorous hint," then springing the trap on them. But it never brutalizes them; its irony is never heavy and cutting, as is the satiric irony of Ben Jonson.[49] To Sheridan, the smiles of good comic invention are only "half-triumphant."

Sheridan's arguments against sentimental comedy, all of them posited in the tenth-night prologue to *The Rivals*, advance four premises: (1) that, since pure comedy is itself fully able "To charm the fancy and yet reach the heart," sentimental comedy really adds nothing to the tested stock of dramatic art; (2) that sentimental comedy so refines and perfects human motives as to deny all semblance of reality to the major characters of the play; (3) that all comedy, sentimental or otherwise, rests on a thematic structure too light to support heavy moral preachments; and (4) that morality taught in defense of high virtue properly emerges from tragedy and tragedy only. Although Sheridan does not explicitly echo Goldsmith's warning that sentimental comedy might one day kill pure comedy altogether, Mrs. Bulkley does predict that the sentimental Muse will one day snatch the poignard from the hands of tragedy and violently do to death all the leading comic actors of Covent Garden Theatre.

Anyone seeing Sheridan's prologues and epilogues as reliable keys to his dramatic theory might well heed Mary Etta Knapp's warning that prologue writers, especially those who were also theater patentees and managers, often yielded more readily to popular expedience than to the demands of systematic literary theory.[50] Garrick, for example, so fully committed himself to pleasing the audience that his prologues and epilogues, one-hundred-sixty of them yet surviving, advance no consistent literary theory. It might at least be said, however, that Sheridan introduces no inconsistencies into the dramatic theory developed in his prologues and epilogues (perhaps because so few of them treat of esthetic subjects), nor does his practice as playwright anywhere seriously contradict this theory. Of course, his practice goes considerably beyond his theory; for he subtly manipulates the effects and qualities of laughter, colors and controls the degrees of comic amiability, and governs the force and direction of satiric thrusts. But, in both comedy and tragedy, Sheridan remains essentially faithful to his theory — so far as his theory goes.

V The Critic: *Dramaturgy*

Through the burlesque action of his last significant comedy, *The Critic* (1779), Sheridan offers his own comment on the craft of play making. And, while he certainly develops no new dramaturgical schemes, he at least reveals a keen awareness of the problems playwrights face. In the second and third acts of *The Critic*, Mr. Puff, a journalist-turned-playwright, directs the first rehearsal of his new tragedy "The Spanish Armada." He fashions his play according to rules and practices deduced from contemporary theater, the tragedies he has seen performed, and each of his rules and practices provides a negative precept for the careful playwright's art.

Puff's own shabby exposition, for example, as well as his practice of having two characters discuss with one another a situation already obviously known to them both, affirms Sheridan's view that exposition must be realistically motivated and carefully and logically presented.[51] Puff's assumption that the audience should be grateful for whatever information it can get, and through whatever means (220), suggests Sheridan's insistence upon closely detailed and clearly drawn exposition. And, through Puff's declaration that exposition requires plain language while other dialogue allows "trope, figure, and metaphor, as plenty as noun-substantives" (220), Sheridan implies that florid set speeches should not influence the language and order of a play, thereby loading the narrative progress with fancy rhetorical excrescences.

Other Puff "rules" reflect Sheridan's disdain for bad plotting: for love interests arbitrarily hitched onto the action of a history play (215), for subplots completely unrelated to main plots (229), for the tradition itself of spinning out multiple plots when one plot will serve much better (229). They also reflect his distaste for hackneyed stage conventions, the customary music for the customary entrance, the customary costume for the customary action, all the worn-out stage business represented in Puff's presentation of his heroine: her soft introductory music, her mad scene in white satin, the awkward confidante who shadows her everywhere (238). Since Puff's rules derive from widespread theatrical practice, they best serve to explode the abuse of convention; and through them Sheridan broadens his complaints to include (1) the use of dazzling stage effects at the expense of dialogue, (2) the over-protracted preparation of stage entrances, (3) the incorporation of unnecessary stock scenes, (4) the use of stock metaphors in poetic dialogue, (5) the reversion to such facile tactics as "poetical second-sight" in which "a hero or heroine, in consideration of their being often obliged to overlook things that *are* on the stage, is allow'd to hear and see a number of things that are not."[52] Especially when considered alongside Puff's wildly irresponsible practices — shabby exposition, unmotivated entrances and exits, atrocious language — his rules constitute a truly impressive catalogue of dramaturgical offenses. And they provide inversely a striking catalogue of dramaturgical principles.

These principles rest upon the same basis of judgment that supports Sheridan's poetic theory. They show little respect for fixed rules; and they show major concern for common sense logic, for what reason dictates as the most apposite strategy for a given dramatic effect. Certainly Sheridan's practice as playwright is not anti-conventionalist. In characterization and situation, he owes an immense debt to convention. But the satire of *The Critic* emphasizes that convention must be adapted tactfully and logically, not arbitrarily, and that all the problems of motivation and organization raised by the play must be solved responsibly and imaginatively. To Sheridan, playmaking was obviously a serious and exacting business.

CHAPTER 3

Poet

W HETHER penning a sweet love lyric to Eliza, or dashing off a song for performance at the theater, or acknowledging some special occasion, great or small, Sheridan always displayed a bright flair for versifying. Excluding the songs in his major plays, his poetic canon includes at least sixty titles; and these poems embrace an immense variety of forms and subjects and obviously constitute a substantial segment of Sheridan's literary achievement.

I *Poetic Satire: "The Ridotto of Bath"*

Quite possibly he broke into print as a poet on May 9, 1771, with the publication in *The Bath Chronicle* of "Hymen and Hirco: A Vision," a rather bland "Juvenalian" satire attacking Walter Long, the aging Wiltshire squire who for a time was contracted to marry Elizabeth Linley, Sheridan's own future bride. But a poem quite definitely Sheridan's appeared in *The Bath Chronicle* on October 10, 1771: "The Ridotto of Bath, a Panegyrick, Being an Epistle from Timothy Screw, Under Server to Messrs. Kuhf and Fitzwater, to his brother Henry, Waiter at Almack's." The little poem satirizes the opening ball at the New Assembly Rooms of Bath — an occasion gloriously celebrated just ten days earlier on September 30 — and, in doing so, it cleverly imitates the eleventh and thirteenth letters of Christopher Anstey's roistering verse novel, the *New Bath Guide* (1766). Executed in the anapestic couplets popularized for satire by Anstey, it also features, as one critic notes, "the same chit-chat, the same mild, laughing satire upon modish follies, the same snobbishness about social risers, and even the same 'character' naming" typical of the *Guide* — e.g., Tom Handleflask, Miss Churchface, Madame Crib'em, Peg Runt.[1] Young Sheridan obviously hoped to use the credit of Anstey's popularity, but his imitation reflects an appropriate artistic tact; for by 1771 the *Guide* widely symbolized the reckless mood of Bath gaiety.

The chief merit of the "Ridotto of Bath" appears in its structure. After two brief preliminary sections, events proceed chronologically from seven in the evening, when the gala begins, to one in the morning, when everyone goes home; but, within the framework of this simple structure, the poet generates a system of delightful dramatic tensions and leads through them to a final, rowdy climax. Tensions take hold even at the outset where the narrator, a veteran waiter, declares this ridotto to be the grandest of his long experience. A mock ominousness compounds these tensions when in his second brief prefatory comment the narrator tells how the Mayor of Bath, on hearing that the new entertainment parlors will house a "Red Otter," threatens to cancel the grand opening. And the sense of foreboding generated by this threat takes emphasis, in turn, from the earliest description of the guests attending the ridotto, many of whom have ignored the regulations for dress specified by the master of ceremonies. Thus tensions inherent in the grandness of the affair are immediately heightened by the threat of cancellation and by signs of social anarchy within the company.

The climax toward which these tensions build is the assault upon the sideboard, which takes place in the long penultimate section of the poem. It is a climax prepared by a descriptive passage confirming in close detail the reader's worst fears about the company assembled: an undisciplined mob, highlighted by the glitter of cheap paste jewelry, mixing low and polite society, dancing grotesquely to the lilting jigs of oboe and fiddle. To elevate his climax even above this chaos of merriment, Sheridan introduces a dramatic pause into the narrative: the din subsides; the music stops; order presides. But out of this disconcerting silence soon rumbles a crushing stampede. Dinner is served:

> Our outworks they storm'd with prowess most manful,
> And jellies and cakes carried off by the handful;
> While some our lines enter'd, with courage undaunted,
> Nor quitted the trench till they'd got what they wanted. (122)[2]

Although the closing section of the poem covers a sizable segment of time — from the dinner hour to one o'clock in the morning — it is itself quite brief, a foreshortened denouement to the little narrative. In it, the narrator mentions the continuing "*folly, confusion,* and *pathos*" of the ridotto; but he describes no action and generates no tension. He does nothing to dissipate the impact of the chaotic dining room scene. From beginning to end, Sheridan sustains the structural integrity of his poem, always supplying detail and controlling tensions in careful support of a single, riotous climax.

Unfortunately, very little within the poem supports its effective structure. The narrative *persona*, Timothy Screw, assumes no clear identity, though he postures after a studied comic diffidence. The young poet's ventures into dialect humor *("Red Otter"* for "ridotto," *"Hogstyegon"* for "octagon," *"purdigiously"* for "prodigiously," *"suffocking"* for "suffocating") fare feebly at best; and his anapests stumble badly at times, e.g., "In sympathy beat the balcony above" (121). The mere thought of a grand Bath ball, says Anstey's Simkin Bernard, "Gives life to my numbers, and strength to my verse." Sheridan's Timothy Screw professes a comparable enthusiasm, but his numbers and verse fail to reflect it.

Despite its failings, however, "The Ridotto of Bath" earned popularity sufficient to enshrine it in the *New Foundling Hospital for Wit* (1771), a widely circulated anthology of current verse; and, by virtue of Sheridan's fine sense of drama and form, the little poem clearly elevates itself above mere "trifle" and "commonplace."[3] In being satire, of course, it ranks low on Sheridan's own scale of theoretical values — the values he suggests in his later poems "Clio's Protest" (1771) and "A Familiar Epistle" (1774). But, even while warning in these poems against the dangers of satire, he demonstrates in them as lively a satiric turn of mind as he demonstrates in "The Ridotto of Bath." Certainly "Clio's Protest" shows a mastery of Hudibrastic techniques — the driving pace, the extravagant rhymes, the casual tone, the sporadic asides, the studied digressions — and "A Familiar Epistle" sees these same techniques sharpened and intensified after the manner of Charles Churchill: the feminine endings dramatically reduced, the tone perceptibly darkened, the sense of order more systematically asserted. In these two poems, as in "The Ridotto," the young poet has major problems with the syntax, which is loose and sometimes contrived, and in the phrasal excesses which drain many lines of their rhetorical energy and graphic interest. At the same time, however, all three poems reflect his metrical and dictional versatility and his keen ear for parody and imitation. Despite his theoretical distaste for satire, Sheridan was an effective verse satirist from the start.

II *Fugitive Verse*

Long ago Ernest Rhys concluded that "no song or lyric can hope to reach the ear of the common people which cannot draw, as the old folksongs did, on the congenial living rhythms of its own day."[4]

Sheridan's essential poetic embraces this concept, and his sharp ear
for the congenial living rhythms of his day gave rise to many an easy
occasional poem. Shaping his taste for lyric verse, according to
Sichel, was Sheridan's schoolboy experience with Horace,
Theocritus, and Anacreon; but chiefly he immersed himself in the
seventeenth-century love songs of Jonson and his school. "He stood
on a lower plane than most of the Cavalier lyrists," writes Sichel,
"but none the less on a plane distinguished of its kind. And he
moved there with rambling footsteps."[5]

These footsteps ranged widely among lyric metrical reaches,
traversing puckish anacreontics, lambent dactyls, lilting anapests,
close-cropped iambs, a splendid variety of song-book measures,
often used in intricate combinations, always fashioned to "read
themselves into harmony," after Sheridan's characteristic manner.
Taken all-in-all (Rhodes collects thirty-seven in his edition), they
meet virtually every specification prescribed for good occasional
poetry by Frederick Locker-Lampson, the acknowledged master of
vers de société. For the most part, they are "graceful, refined, and
fanciful, not seldom distinguished by chastened sentiment, and
often playful." Their rhyme is "frequent and never forced." They
are marked by "tasteful moderation, high finish and completeness";
and they project a wide spectrum of attitudes and tones: "whimsically sad," "gay and gallant," "playfully malicious," "tenderly
ironical," "satirically facetious." They are rarely "flat, or ponderous,
or commonplace"; and they are often graced with important
"qualities of brevity and buoyancy."[6]

Sheridan's love lyrics, most of them products of his courtship with
Elizabeth Linley, not only represent the largest corpus of his occasional verse but also exemplify his best lyric craftsmanship.
Although many of them spring from autobiographical roots, they
carefully employ the conventional generic idiom, masking personal
identities behind such pastoral names as Delia, Sylvio, Eliza, and
Damon. And, while Sheridan certainly lived his personal love in-
tensely, he remains artist enough to perceive the nicest dramatic
potential of a love experience and to exercise over his poems a con-
trolled emotional detachment. The psychological ironies of love obviously fascinate him: that in the blush of youth lovers should con-
template death, that the most intense affection is liable to transien-
cy, that the most innocent and well-intentioned love-counsel can
provoke rebuff, and that a "dear delight" companions love-despair.
Sheridan seeks no logical resolution to such ironies; instead, he con-

trives a miniature play, a sensitive little melodrama, in which the speaker tells someone (or something) about the curious awareness love has sparked in him. The distance separating the speaker from his audience varies from poem to poem, for sometimes, as in "We Two, Each Other's Only Pride" (240), the auditor seems close at hand, ready to reply. At other times, as in "To the Recording Angel" (231), he seems far removed but spiritually accessible. At yet other times, as in "On the Death of Elizabeth Linley" (251), the tiny drama unfolds in solemn soliloquy, not self-indulgent but affecting, the pastoral names tactfully put aside.

Just as the love poems are more often experiential than argumentative, they are often more declarative than pictorial. In "The Grotto," for example, where the despairing speaker addresses first the "grotto of moss cover'd stone" then the "willow with leaves dripping dew" (232), the physical details function less as images than as agents of dialogue. Much the same concept governs the physical detail in "To Elizabeth Linley" in which the earnest Sylvio threatens to "hate flowers, elms, sweet bird, and grove" unless Eliza now sings to him the songs she has sung earlier to the woods and trees. The charming lyric "To Laura" — which vacillates irregularly between four- and five-line ballad stanzas, concluding in a stanzaic couplet — again finds a pensive speaker addressing the Nature he sees and feels; yet here the dramatic setting assumes a clarity unusual for Sheridan, picturing "a willow of no vulgar size," with shady boughs and roots providing a "moss-grown seat," the tree's bark "shatter'd" (as the poet puts it) by the inscription of Laura's name. Fretted further with emphatic images of an "azure" sky, "rosy-ting'd" sunbeams, and the "roseate wings" of May, the poem offers the most highly particularized imagery in Sheridan's love verse (possibly excepting "On the Death of Elizabeth Linley"); and it suggests at the same time how small a role pictorial details play in the total effect of his lyricism. With comparable generality he celebrates in other love lyrics his lady's "eye of heav'nly blue" and her "cheek of roseate hue." Obviously embarrassed by such formulaic descriptions, he succeeds best at lampooning them, as he does in an anacreontic beginning "I ne'er could any lustre see/In eyes that would not look on me" (225), a poem rivaling convention in the spirit of Shakespeare's Sonnet 130.

Most of the best qualities of Sheridan's love-lyricism appear in a sensitive three-stanza lyric "Dry Be That Tear," probably dating to the courtship period, 1770 - 72. According to Moore, this poem

smacks of a French madrigal by Gibert de Montreuil, who probably
had it from an Italian song by Gilles de Ménage; but Sheridan likely
took the sentiment from David Hume's essay "The Epicurean,"
Hume having got it from Continental sources.[7] The first stanza runs
as follows:

> Dry be that tear, my gentlest love,
>   Be hush'd that struggling sigh,
> Nor seasons, day, nor fate shall prove
>   More fix'd, more true than I.
> Hush'd be that sigh, be dry that tear,
> Cease boding doubt, cease anxious fear. —
>   Dry be that tear.

These lines suggest again that Sheridan's lyric imagination is aural,
not visual; that it is declarative, not argumentative. As Sichel
suggests, the poem "sets itself to music by the rise and fall of its
melody."[8] Through patterns of repetition, it seems to savor its own
sounds; its medial pauses and parallel phrases govern the tempo and
sustain soft overtones even to the final muted echo: "Dry be that
tear." The remaining two stanzas evince the same closely disciplined
rhetoric, the same balanced phrasal patterns (modulated as here by
varying accentual meters), the same six-line ballad scheme (*ababcc*)
with the bobbed tail-rhyme redolent of Sir Thomas Wyatt's "My
Lute Awake!" Perhaps it bears saying here that the opening lines of
this lyric were borrowed from a "Dwarf Elegy on a Lady of Middle
Age" by Nathaniel Brassey Halhed.[9] They so struck Sheridan's fancy
that he repeated them in 1795 at the outset of an "Elegy on the
Death of a British Officer," a poem printed with "Clio's Protest" in
1819 under the title "Verses Addressed to Laura" and beginning
"Scarce hush'd the sigh, scarce dried the [lingering] tear."

Fugitive poems not treating of love turn like the love lyrics upon
subtly ironic situations, but they do so quite whimsically and often
quite satirically. Again the concepts are largely declarative, not
closely analyzed, not logically resolved nor imaged forth. And again
many a light irony tickles the poet's fancy: an urbane lady complains
that the birds in Hyde Park trouble her with country sounds (241);
the founder of Brooks's Club, a great moneylender, pays at last his
own moral mortgage in heaven (248); Lady Anne Hamilton, indulged in every luxury, laments her "sad" human lot (253); two eminent speakers of the House of Commons lie together dead as they
had "lied" living. By technical devices Sheridan touches such ironies

as these with just the right twinkling of an eye, just the right hint of a smile. Thus he lets the super-urbanized Hyde Park lady speak for herself, ingenuously, in sweeping anapests (his second use of Anstey's measure), gaily effusing the innocent vacuity of *bon ton* taste. In the "Epitaph on Brooks," he mixes lugubrious tones with irreverent jingle measures. He uses separated anapestic couplets to catalogue the bright good fortunes of Lady Anne Hamilton, ending each second line with the playful phrase "—— poor Anne." And, in mock incantation, as though a hymn were parodied, he eulogizes the two dead speakers of the House of Commons: "Mourn, mourn, St. Stephen's Choirs with ceaseless grieving/Two kindred spirits from the senate fled" (249).

The nice perception enabling Sheridan to define subtle social ironies also sharpens his delight in trivia — a delight inspiring, for example, a gentle mock elegy on the death of his wife's avadavat. "Each bird that is born of an egg has its date," the little poem soulfully admits. But so special a bird as this one, schooled to its song by Elizabeth's own sweet voice, will surely outsing every Muse in heaven (249). Other poems celebrating great conflicts born of trivial things include "Lines By a Lady on the Loss of Her Trunk," an Anstey's measure in which each terminal word rhymes with "trunk" until the poem exhausts itself for want of available rhymes (254), and "The Walse," which coolly attributes the waltz step, introduced into England in 1812, to the craftiness of the devil who had contrived that a gentleman's hand should rest upon a lady's hip, even in public (257).

In other fugitive poems, Sheridan displays a fine flair for patriotic verse and a gift for lively political caricature. As a patriotic versifier, for example, he composed on a moment's notice two rousing songs for an interlude to *Harlequin Fortunatus*, a pantomime produced at Drury Lane on January 3, 1780. Both these songs develop the *dulce et decorum* theme: one heartens the lonely midnight watch to thoughts of glory; the other braces the soldiers at the ramparts and rings the resolute chorus "Britons, strike home revenge your country's wrong" (239). This instinct for patriotic bravura also gives rise to a much-celebrated stanza written impromptu and appended to the National Anthem to be sung at Drury Lane in special tribute to the King, who that very evening (in 1800) had narrowly escaped assassination at the theater.

As political caricaturist, Sheridan dabbled "at various dates" in a few pasquinades, impaling on the point of a rusty doggerel those political figures whose names fell naturally into swinging anapests or amphibracs: "Johnny W---lks, Johnny W---lks;" "Jack Ch---ch---ll, Jack Ch---ch---ll;" "Captain K---th, Captain K---th," etc. (259 - 60). According to Crompton Rhodes, the rough-hewn, eight-line stanzas, a discrete scattering of them found among Sheridan's papers, fit the melody of a popular air beginning "Mistress Arne, Mistress Arne/It gives me concarn."[10] And while, as Moore long ago remarked, time has "removed their venom, and with it, in a great degree, their wit,"[11] the faded caricatures still suggest the writer's true eye for his subjects' foibles and his true aim in striking them down. Sheridan's real merit as a character poet, however, endures in "A Portrait for Amoret," a splendid panegyric upon Mrs. Frances Crewe.

III   Verse Portraiture: "A Portrait for Amoret"

"A Portrait for Amoret" was written as a prefatory compliment to be bound with a handsome manuscript copy of The School for Scandal presented by Sheridan to Mrs. Crewe soon after the play was introduced on May 8, 1777. Correspondence between Lord Camden and David Garrick indicates that the poem was in circulation within four months after the first performance of the play,[12] but it did not appear in print until much later, and then surreptitiously, causing Sheridan, when he saw it, to remark in a letter to his second wife that Nature had made him in his youth "an ardent romantic Blockhead."[13]

By all contemporary accounts, the incomparable Frances Crewe, only daughter of Fulke Greville, readily fired the ardor of many a fawning macaroni; but Sheridan's poem is really quite restrained and is perhaps the more ardent for its restraint. It develops in four parts: (1) an invocation to the Daughters of Calumny, promising to portray for them a lady unassailable by slander; (2) invocations to Mrs. Crewe herself ("Amoret") and to the Muse who must portray her; (3) the portrait of Amoret, which treats in turn of her splendid bearing, her captivating manner, her arresting modesty, her intriguing lips, her tactfully "irresolute" eyes, her killing smile, her ready wit, her diffident manner ("female doubt"), her spritely heart, her taste for mirth, her refined raillery, her "scorn of folly," and her high respect for talent; and (4) a grudging concession by the Daughters of Calumny that the lady portrayed, finally identified as Mrs. Crewe, does indeed defy all slander and envy.

Certainly Crompton Rhodes is right in complaining that the prac-

tice of printing Mrs. Crewe's name immediately beneath the title of
the poem, a practice apparently customary in editions earlier than
his own,[14] destroys the rhetorical conceit intended by Sheridan.
Rhodes is right, too, in maintaining that the poem does not, as Sichel
and others have held,[15] credit Mrs. Crewe with inspiring *The School
for Scandal*, although the "adepts at Scandal's School" in the poem
suggest the Scandal College of the play, especially as to types and
varieties of scandalmongering. Quite irrespective of the play, it is
Mrs. Crewe alone who has "cast a fatal gloom o'er Scandal's reign"
(205). Sheridan specifies this emphasis not only by omitting from the
poem all direct reference to *The School for Scandal* but also, and
most importantly, by building the poem around an extended
suspense conceit. Throughout all four structural segments, he
withholds the true identity of his celebrated subject, heightening interest through the cumulative details of the picture. Only with the
last word of the poem, spoken after an emphatic pause, does he cast
aside her fictive name: "Thee my inspirer; and my model —
CREWE!" And thus emphatically does he complete the portrait.

It is important to bear in mind, of course, that his device is for
suspense, not for surprise. The terminal word satisfies expectation; it
does not shock or outrage it. Once "A Portrait for Amoret" is completed, the reader delights that he has played the game of rhetorical
suspense, and he then returns to the poem — as to any completed
portrait — to delight further in its textures and lineaments. In view
of Sheridan's liberal theories of prosody, "A Portrait" is the more interesting for its closely disciplined meter. It is written in heroic
couplets of a highly restrictive sort. Caesuras fall customarily after
the fourth, fifth, or sixth syllables. Most of the rhyming terms are
"action words," either verbs or verbals, long in pronunciation.
Although many shades of verbal coloring suggest themselves,
Sheridan does not allow music to smother sense. Each narrow cell of
sense takes interest from its own distinctive rhetoric, contributing to
a rich variety of balanced constructions — sometimes with an-
tithesis, sometimes by echo, sometimes between equal parts, showing two stressed accents on each side a medial pause, sometimes
between unequal parts, showing two stressed accents on one side the
pause and three on the other. Variety derives, too, from phrasal se-
quences, from intricate systems of repetition, from the echo of initial
terms. But, amidst all this variety, the formal identity of the heroic
couplet remains strong: there is virtually no enjambment between
couplets.

If Sheridan still felt in 1777, as he had felt in 1771, that versification should closely complement the subject versified, it perhaps seems curious that so formal a meter should serve the subject of this poem. But since, as Wallace Cable Brown remarks, the heroic couplet is the most rigid poetic form, it is also the form in which "the greatest variations are possible without destroying the basic pattern."[16] As Sheridan pictures Mrs. Crewe, then, the strict heroic couplet is an ideal metrical form. Within the tight framework of its basic pattern — both stanzaically and structurally — the exciting variety of Mrs. Crewe's character scintillates in the rhetorical variety of the verse.

The closing couplets of the poem mention color and outline: "And lo! each pallid hag, with blister'd tongue . . . Owns all the colours just; the outline true" (11. 121, 123), but apart from rhetorical and verbal effects, few colors or outlines really appear. What does appear is a careful modulation of tones, starting with the brusque and irritable apostrophe to the Daughters of Calumny (with the sharp imperative "Attend!" repeated at the outset of four couplets). Following, then, is tonal modulation to the quiet invocation of Amoret "Come, gentle Amoret . . . Come" (11. 25, 27). Afterward the portrait itself takes form, not in sensory detail, but in verbal tones and rhetorical schemes, helping to delineate the personal qualities of the lady portrayed. Here is a representative passage:

> Adorning Fashion, unadorn'd by dress,
> Simple from taste, and not from carelessness;
>
> Discreet in gesture, in deportment mild
> Not stiff with prudence, nor uncouthly wild;
>
> No state has Amoret! no studied mien;
> She frowns *no goddess*, and she moves *no queen*. (202)

It is the *simplex munditiis* convention again, managed here much more successfully than in the translations. In the first two of the couplets, the balanced four-stress lines, joined in each case by an unaccented syllable or by a monosyllabic "low" word (as Tillotson labels the device),[17] point in their rhetoric a simple elegance complimenting Amoret's bearing. The third couplet, which shifts to a negative emphasis, properly accents the negative terms in its scansion, most strongly stressing in each line the single iterative term "no," and thus really accenting only two syllables a line.

The shift in rhetoric, then, accompanies the shift in descriptive emphasis. In other words, rhetorical and verbal coloring help to delineate personal quality. And it is worth reiterating that Sheridan favors throughout the poem qualities of character over physical detail. The blush in Amoret's cheek betokens her modesty; her lips and eyelids move at the bidding of love; her taste for mirth bespeaks a contemplative mind. These and other high qualities receive form and vitality through apt tonal and rhetorical variations; and, in this tonal and rhetorical sense, the reader, like the Daughters of Calumny, must "Own the colours just; the outline true."

IV *Theatrical Monody: "Verses to the Memory of Garrick"*

A second of Sheridan's major poems — his "Verses to the Memory of Garrick" (1779) — also features tight heroic couplets; and again the poem achieves remarkable variety within the limitations of its medium. This time, however, Sheridan calls more deliberately upon a subtle principle of metrical tensions — one serving to heighten the dramatic effects of oral presentation. In his study of English prosody in the eighteenth century, Paul Fussell sees this principle as originating in 1745 with Samuel Say's *Poems on Several Occasions*. It recognizes two levels of scansion in the poetic line — one based on actual sense stress, the other on theoretical or artificial stress — and holds that prosodic pleasures derive from a continuing conflict between the two levels. Where they coincide, no prosodic tensions develop; but, where they pull apart, tensions, and the consequent prosodic pleasures, result.[18] Sheridan seems to suggest this concept in his unfinsihed treatise on prosody, in which he insists that "A verse should read itself into harmony," asserting its own "actual rithm," but adds that "we may vary the accent as we please and the propriety is in doing so melodiously."[19] Writing in 1775, Thomas Sheridan states the concept in yet another way by declaring that "to render numbers for any time pleasing to the ear, variety is as essential as uniformity"; and he adds that "the highest ornament of versification arises from disparity in the members, equality in the whole."[20] Both the Sheridans echo Say's call for "a proper Mixture of Uniformity and Variety" to effect prosodic tension.[21]

Although written in eleven stanzas of varying lengths, the monody on Garrick falls into four distinct organizational segments; and their content suggests the discrete portions of a Classical oration. In the first, an *exordium* (11.1 - 20), the speaker points the aptness of this tribute to Garrick, a tribute properly paid here in the great actor's own theater. The second, a kind of *narratio* (ll. 21 - 62), considers acting in relation to painting, sculpture, and poetry; and it concludes that of all these arts only acting stands vulnerable to time. The third, a *confirmatio* (ll. 63 - 78), defines in sequence the qualities of the actor's art and proves the ephemerality of these qualities. The fourth, a *peroratio* (ll. 79 - 112), urges Garrick's admirers to immortalize his artistry in their memories, since of itself it lacks enduring substance. Contemporary periodical sources indicate that "airs of a solemn nature" twice interrupt the theatrical reading of the poem.[22] The first, a setting of lines nine and ten, embellishes the *exordium;* the second, following line seventy-eight, introduces the *peroratio* (perhaps covering lines 79 through 83 as set off stanzaically in the text). The elder Thomas Linley scored these interludes, introducing into them a variety of choruses, airs, and vocal ensembles. He also composed special instrumental pieces to precede and follow the recitation. Printed in four quarto pages, the music was probably sold at the theater; but it had not the distribution, certainly, that the text of the monody had.

As published by T. Evans and others late in March, 1779, the text of the monody provides several clear signals to metrical emphasis — reduced capitals, contractions, marked caesuras, exclamation points, expletives — devices showing where the poem's theoretical scansion must be observed and where it must not. The *exordium*, for example, features a close marriage of spoken and theoretical scansions, contractions often cementing the marriage, as in line four: "For fabled Suffe'rers, and delusive Woe."[23] Those portions of the *narratio* treating of painting and sculpture also cling to prosodic wedlock, though a capitalized "HIS WORKS" in line twenty-eight offers to shatter the bond: "With undiminish'd Awe HIS WORKS are view'd." In the third part of the *narratio* (the discourse on poetry), however, a prosodic tension takes hold, signaled by pronounced caesuras and trochaic substitutions as well as by reduced capitals: "The Pride of Glory — Pity's Sigh sincere — " (l. 53); "Such is THEIR Meed, THEIR Honors thus secure" (l.55). And this tension heralds the emotive climax of the piece: the *confirmatio* and the early portions of the *peroratio* (ll. 63 - 78; 83 - 92).

Since the poem seeks throughout to be logically persuasive, it is nowhere passionate or irrational. In the *confirmatio*, however, it engages a pathos commensurate with the irony of the actor's lot. It defines in turn the qualities of his art — grace of action, adopted mien, expressive glance, gesture, harmonious speech — at last bringing the catalogue to this effective conclusion (ll. 73 - 78).

PASSION'S wild break, — and FROWN that awes the Sense,
And every CHARM of gentler ELOQUENCE —
All perishable! — like the 'Electric Fire
But strike the Frame — and as they strike expire;
Incense too pure a bodied Flame to bear,
It's Fragrance charms the Sense, and blends with Air.

Moore writes that certain of Sheridan's friends urged him to alter line seventy-five, causing the emphatic phrase "All perishable!" to read "All doomed to perish."[24] And, in refusing to make the change, Sheridan suggests the deliberate care with which he blends uniformity and variety not only here but at apt places throughout the poem. A wealth of metrical variety suggests itself even in these few lines quoted.

The trochaic patterns enforced by the initial terms "PASSION'S" and "Incense," for example, precisely recall the fundamental technique of "variety in uniformity" as urged in Thomas Sheridan's lectures on reading. So do the hovering medial pauses, marked typographically by the dash, and the "demicaesuras" synchronized with them to introduce "a diversity of proportion in the measurement of the pauses" (cf. 11. 73. and 76).[25] The celebrated seventy-fifth line, moreover, demonstrates in the opening phrase ("All perishable!") the intermixture of spondees and pyrrhics, a device for variety much admired by the elder Sheridan; and, in its closing phrase (" — like the 'Electric Fire"), the line engages a medial trochee calculated, as Thomas Sheridan would interpret it, to shatter melody while heightening expression.[26]

In short, appropriate variety characterizes the entire poem. The more coolly rational passages show least prosodic tension; the more emotionally excited ones place proper oral scansion at odds with regular iambic cadence. Verbal coloring everywhere supports prosodic effects — cf, "the Meed of mournful Verse" (1. 11); "Pity's sigh sincere" (1. 53) "with Force and Feeling fraught" (1. 67) — but here, as in the "Portrait for Amoret," the figurism remains much more rhetorical than sensuous. The poem always asserts its own integrity, its "actual rithm." At appropriate times, however, it signals the reader to "vary the accent," to violate the prosodic surface, to cooperate with the poetry — but not to overwhelm it — in evoking apt dramatic response.

In staging the monody as introduced at Drury Lane on March 11, 1779, Sheridan probably imitated the production ten years earlier of Garrick's own *Ode Upon Dedicating a Building and Erecting a*

Statue to Shakespeare at Stratford-upon-Avon, for just as the ode featured choristers banked behind a statue of Shakespeare, with the reader (Garrick) and several soloists stationed in the foreground, so the monody featured a choir arranged "as at oratorios,"[27] with the tragic actress Mary Ann Yates standing center-forward to read the poem beside a portrait of Garrick. Except for these superficial details of production, however, the two poems are vastly unlike; for while Garrick constantly shifted the metrical pace of his poem, following the tradition of the cantata ode, Sheridan patiently plied his heroic couplets, finding metrical variety and dramatic tension in the prosodic resources of the verse.

The monody held the boards for ten performances[28] — certainly a creditable record for a funeral oration, especially in that Garrick's jubilee ode could manage only eight. And when in 1816 Lord Byron's monody on Sheridan was read at Drury Lane, its close metrical imitation of Sheridan's poem clearly attested to Byron's view that the monody on Garrick was the best "address" in the language.[29]

V   The Prologues and Epilogues as Poetry

Considering Sheridan's prologues and epilogues among thousands of others, Mary Etta Knapp leaves no question that he closely embraced presiding convention in them. According with convention, he generally thought of prologues and epilogues as being dramatic presentations separate and distinct from the plays they preceded or followed. In composing them, he shamelessly pilfered weary conventional conceits. He warmed over many a stale and moldy theme, apparently always ready (despite the merit of the case he pleaded) to curry favor from an audience usually innocent of clear judgment and often jaded of taste. In short, Sheridan nowhere belies Miss Knapp's comfortable generalization that "the prologues and epilogues of the eighteenth century are characteristic of their own time, reflecting the minutiae of daily life, presenting the difficulties and triumphs of the theatre, obeying changes in taste, recording in a lively manner social and dramatic history."[30]

At the same time, however, Sheridan's pieces engage the Classic paradox of prologue writing. As Miss Knapp herself notes, and as she quotes Henry Fielding as noting in his day, the work of individual prologue-epilogue writers often asserts a striking distinctiveness, even though the general conceptual detail of their work may be largely conventional.[31] Such, certainly, is Sheridan's case. His prologues and epilogues — only twelve in sum — add little leaven to the lump; but they clearly outline his assessment of the genre itself, suggesting his views (1) that prologues and epilogues must acknowledge the privileged position of the audience; (2) that their rhetoric is usually persuasive; (3) that their office is usually instructive; and (4) that they thrive upon formal and thematic convention.

In acknowledging the privileged position of the audience, Sheridan's prologues and epilogues see the playgoers as critics in spite of themselves. They have come to the theater to be entertained; but they seem, from the poet's point of view, to have no clear idea what constitutes good entertainment. The amorphous, corporate judgment they assert needs difinition; so the prologues and epilogues define the judgment. In effect, they tell the audience what it likes and why it likes what it likes, thus to contrive a union of interests (more or less specific) between the playgoers and the play they are about to see or have just seen. Actually, then, the poet maintains authority over his audience, even as he acknowledges the audience's privileged position as critic *malgré lui.* Sheridan naturally delights in this sort of psychological situation; and (at least after the success of his first play) he exploits it delightfully by quite coolly manipulating the distance between his audience and the speaker of his piece.

His earliest fully extant prologue, for example (that for the second night of *The Rivals,* January 28, 1775), is an acting piece spoken between a sergeant-at-law and an attorney.[32] Its scenic point of view and its rather formal concluding set speech, in which the sergeant pleads the young poet's brief, hold the audience at a respectful distance and seek favor through cautious and tentative flattery, as befits the precarious position of a beginner whose first play owes its second performance wholly to the extraordinary indulgence of a sympathetic first-night jury. Even in this tentativeness, however, the poet (through his solicitor) declares the audience (jury) his friend, promises that he seeks only to please, insists that he values good criticism, and utterly disarms hostility by placing the playgoers in a constructive critical position. In effect, he invites the playgoers to coauthorship with him in the play, thus subtly sharing with them responsibility for its success and its failure. They are therefore much inclined to admire its merits and to minimize its weaknesses, especially since this second performance (given eleven days after the first and revised in response to first-night criticism) reflects the young poet's sincerity in seeking their friendly aid.

His case at last favorably decided, he greets his tenth-night audience with a new and warmly intimate prologue[33] spoken by Mrs. Bulkley, who plays Julia Melville in the production; and in it she directly solicits the playgoer's indulgences not for the playwright but for the Muse. Again, however, he acknowledges the privileged position of the audience by having his speaker encourage between playgoers and playwrights a cooperative effort against the usurping bastard, sentimental comedy. He does not dictate taste; he rather defines among friends a cogent detail of good judgment. Such a covert but persistent tact characterizes even the most insolent of his prologues and epilogues.

Thus if the epilogue to *Edward and Eleanora* (1775) assails at the outset the marital indifference of every wife in the audience, it finally rights matters by identifying them all with the martyred heroine of the play and thereby cleverly translates insult into compliment. If the epilogue to *Semiramis* (1776) attacks the demands of taste by offering a serious epilogue after tragedy, rather than the conventional comic one,[34] it disarms criticism by applauding at last the expansive "feeling heart" of the audience. If the epilogue to *The Fatal Falsehood* (1779) fiercely offers to damn the mediocrity of bluestocking scribblers, it finally yields to a proper chivalry and ends with compliments "vastly civil to Female Talent," as Sheridan puts it in a letter to Garrick.[35] Although psychic distance may vary from piece to piece, the controlling decorum is always the same: while honoring the audience's privilege as critic and customer, the poet asserts his own professional authority, subtly shaping the playgoer's judgment after his own.

The rhetoric of such a decorum is perforce persuasive, and the thematic aim is an instructive one. Topics for instruction in Sheridan's prologues and epilogues include not only esthetic matters (see Chapter 2) but also moral and theatrical ones. For example, his prologue to *The Miniature Picture* (1780) points out the difficulties of meeting anticipated production schedules and then deplores the persisting popular taste for imported entertainments.[36] His managerial disgust for foreign art (especially the ballet and the opera) again erupts in the epilogue to *The Fair Circassian* (1781), where he openly laments the high salaries paid foreign performers. Quite conventional in theme, both these pieces instruct the audience to an awareness that imported art poisons the lifeblood of the English theater. On grounds both patriotic and artistic, they champion allegiance to the native stage.

Another theatrical topic, this one treated in an epilogue for a benefit play (undated), teaches the audience that an actor's lot is not a happy one — that for him the verdant springtime, which keeps playgoers out-of-doors and away from benefit performances, is often a bitter winter of the soul. Since each item of instruction implies a consequent obligation, all the prologues and epilogues treating of theatrical matters assert a moral emphasis, a clearly defined implication of oughtness. In effect, they say that playgoers ought to support the native stage, that they ought to sympathize with the manager's scheduling problems, that they ought to attend benefit performances, despite the inviting freshness of the spring. Similarly, the esthetic pieces tell the playgoers what they ought to admire and how they ought to let art — at least some forms of it — enrich their lives.

Sheridan's understanding of the prologue-epilogue genre, his sense of its integrity, apparently presupposes extensive use of formal conventions — the acting piece,[37] the plaintiff-jury metaphor,[38] the practice of having the speaker address each level of the house in turn[39] — but, if convention dominates his work, he personalizes it, as Garrick had done, by topical involvement in it. His own political interests, for example, add substance and vitality to his several uses of the parliamentary metaphor, a structural figure used much like the plaintiff-jury convention in pointing out the judicial and legislative privilege of the audience. Similarly, his career as theater manager enlivens each topical reference to actor and stage; and his career as playwright adds natural vigor to his acting prologues and epilogues.

The persistent liveliness of his work suggests, furthermore, that he embraced convention not for want of imagination but for support of the genre itself. Since he apparently saw thematic and formal convention as nourishing the prologue and epilogue as a poetic type, he sometimes emphasized convention by deliberately departing from it. On the tenth night of *The Rivals*, therefore, he deliberately violates the settled practice of awarding the prologue to a man, underscoring his deliberateness by causing Mrs. Bulkley to declare herself "A female counsel in a female's cause."[40] Consequently, he appeals to convention — the very convention he violates — to emphasize the significance of his theme. He achieves thematic emphasis through a similarly inverse process in the epilogue to *Semiramis* where his self-conscious and openly confessed departure from the conventional comic epilogue (after tragedy) strengthens the high seriousness of his discourse on tragic pathos.

Sheridan moved comfortably, then, within the framework of convention, sometimes personalizing it by involving himself topically in it, sometimes enlarging upon its effects by deliberately departing from it. In at least one detail, moreover, he increased the body of convention itself, adapting to the genre, through his epilogue to Hannah More's *The Fatal Falsehood* (1779), the tradition of the Theophrastian character.[41] This same epilogue, incidentally, offers insight into Sheridan's poetic craftsmanship. His papers yield up a draft of the poem described by Sichel as "no less than one hundred and forty-five unrhymed, unrhythmical lines," a "disjointed farrago" (I, 543). Most of these hobbled measures Sheridan discarded; others he hammered into a Theophrastian portrait cryptically typifying the domestic and artistic ambivalence of the dedicated bluestocking. It is a portrait properly said by Rhodes to be "as consummate in its finish as the neatest raillery of Pope";[42] and, while the poet's conceptual process might well be thought an "uncouth and bewildering way of shaping verse," it is for him an incontestably successful process, as a few representative lines from the poem indicate. They are lines spoken by an indignant male poetaster who is urgently intent on driving *"female* scribblers" from the stage:

> Unfinish'd here an epigram is laid,
> And there, a mantua-maker's bill unpaid;
> Here new-born plays fore-taste the town's applause,
> There, dormant patterns pine for future gauze;
> A moral essay now is all her care,
> A satire next, and then a bill of fare:
> A scene she now projects, and now a dish
> Here's Act the First — and here — Remove with Fish. (276)

Unlike other playwright-prologuists, Sheridan made no gesture to abolish the prologue-epilogue tradition. That the poems bear little relevance to the plays sandwiched between them nowhere distressed his sense of theater. If the genre took roots in the audience's desire for a brief moment of intimacy with the stage, he clearly cooperated in that interest, finding its idiom all but natural to him. Apparently, he honored the tradition as a respectable mode of entertainment, one asserting its own integrity through distinctive and settled conventions and one meriting, by testimony of his achievement in it, a creative effort by no means casual and cheap but everywhere tightly imagined and artistically honest.

CHAPTER 4

The Rivals

A T its first performance, on January 17, 1775, *The Rivals* failed badly. A brilliant audience packed Covent Garden Theatre that night, most of it happily expectant, but some of it primed to heckle. Several disruptive "serpents of envy" got themselves expelled from the galleries before the third act, and a challenge was reported given in the boxes. Critics damned the rude playgoers, but they damned the play even more. They said its plot was unhappily chosen and unskillfully conducted. Its characters lacked novelty. Its witticisms, similes, and metaphors proved but poor substitutes for polished diction. Its materials generally lacked distinctiveness, and it was too long by a full hour. The best of the Covent Garden Company appeared in it — Ned Shuter as Sir Anthony, Henry Woodward as Jack, John Quick as Acres, Lee Lewes as Fag, John Lee as Sir Lucius, Jane Green as Mrs. Malaprop, Jane Barsanti as Lydia, Mary Bulkley as Julia — but, except for Miss Barsanti and Mrs. Bulkley, no one seemed ready to perform; and Shuter and Lee behaved atrociously in their parts. Although a second performance was announced for the eighteenth, the play was judiciously withdrawn, having earned high praise only for the characterizations of Julia and Faulkland, and for a splendid backdrop representing the South Parade at Bath.[1]

I *Revisions*

Before offering the play again on January 28, Sheridan revised it extensively, especially ennobling the character of Sir Lucius O'Trigger, whose original coarseness and stupidity had embarrassed the Irish nation, or so critics held. The first Sir Lucius had approved killing for the joy of it and had taken fortune where he found it, even to the point of marrying Mrs. Malaprop; but the new one approves

65

killing only for "honor" and can discriminate, however slightly, among advantages of fortune. He is largely unoffending.

In fact, most of the alterations made in the play neutralize offensiveness. The original Sir Anthony Absolute — who once passionately threatens to break his own son's jaw and imagines a young lover lying in his mistress' embrace "like a Cucumber on a hot bed" (Larpent, II, 1, p. 47) — emerges in the revision much less violent and goatish. The revised catalogue of Lydia Languish's library suppresses such innuendos as "Roderick Random, and Emily Montagu, under" (Larpent I, 1, p. 10). Mrs. Malaprop's "O he will perforate my Mistery" (Larpent, I, 4, p. 115) becomes "O, he will desolve my mystery," and several of her more unhappy malapropisms are deleted, as is Fag's notorious "meat-for-horses" to mean "metamorphosis."[2]

In redrawing Sir Lucius, in sharpening language, in suppressing ribaldry, Sheridan clearly responded to first-night criticism, just as he did in canceling three whole scenes, in curtailing a fourth (the end of the last act), and in thickening the outlines of Jack Absolute's character. On his own, furthermore, he tightened continuity and heightened comic irony, causing Acres, for example, to tell Absolute of the challenge to Beverley, rather than having the challenge sent by messenger. And, in consequence of such improvements, a play written in six or eight weeks of the summer of 1774[3] reversed after eleven days' revision its discouraging first-night failure. On January 28, all the actors had their parts. Lawrence Clinch brilliantly played the new Sir Lucius, replacing Lee. The revised play triumphed grandly and held the boards for twelve performances between January and June.

II *The Edition of 1775*

The version acted on January 17 (published in 1935 as edited by Richard Little Purdy) survives among the Larpent Manuscripts in the Henry E. Huntington Library. The first issue of the revised play appeared on February 11, 1775, just two weeks after the successful second performance. Curious amplifications in the first printed edition, passages nowhere appearing in the Larpent Manuscript, cause Purdy to suggest that the first edition reinstates matter earlier excised from the Larpent version.[4] Thus the first edition does not represent the precise acting version for January 28. It does, however, preserve the narrative line of that version.

In it, a young army captain named Jack Absolute poses as a half-pay ensign, Ensign Beverley, to woo the capricious heiress Lydia

Languish who is seventeen and rich. But she will lose most of her fortune if she marries without the consent of her aunt, Mrs. Malaprop. In her caprice, she defies her aunt's authority, intending to forfeit her fortune for the love of Beverley, whose poverty and ardor gratify her sense of romance. But, while Jack plies this whimsical Beverley affair, his father, Sir Anthony, proposes him to Mrs. Malaprop as a husband for Lydia, thereby making him his own rival. Two other suitors are also in the field, a country bumpkin named Bob Acres, ironically a good friend of Jack's, who fancies himself wronged by the imaginary Beverley, and Sir Lucius O'Trigger, a petulant Irish baronet who assumes insult from Captain Absolute.

When Lydia at last discovers Jack's true identity, she rejects him sullenly and pouts to think of forfeiting her romantic elopement; and even as he smarts from this rejection he is called onto the dueling field (in each of his identities) to meet Bob Acres and Sir Lucius. Matters are righted, however, when a general alarm brings Sir Anthony and the ladies to the field. The duels are stopped; identities are clarified; and Lydia pities Jack's distress, giving over her caprice for love of him. On discovering that Beverley is really his good friend Jack Absolute, Bob Acres surrenders every claim to Lydia; and, when Sir Lucius — all along duped by Mrs. Malaprop's maid Lucy — discovers that his secret correspondent, his Delia, is really Mrs. Malaprop, he happily withdraws his challenge and so resolves the final rivalry.

The duel scene also resolves the stormy love affair of Julia Melville, Sir Anthony's ward, and a sentimental humorist named Faulkland. So persistently does Faulkland challenge Julia's loyalty, and in such bizarre ways, that she finally dismisses him. But, when she sees him on the dueling field, where he serves as Jack's second, love overcomes prudence and she takes him back. Curiously enough, the Third Edition Corrected — the last edition of *The Rivals* to show Sheridan's further revisions (dated 1776, but actually published in January of 1777) — deletes many passages lacking authority in the Larpent version; but it significantly amplifies the Julia-Faulkland dialogue, as though to strengthen the dramatic responsibility of the secondary plot.

III   *Literary Antecedents to* The Rivals

In the Preface to the 1775 edition, Sheridan declares himself *"by no means conversant with plays in general, either in reading or at the theatre,"* and this ignorance assists him, he says, to avoid *"every appearance of plagiary."*[5] Yet critics have sleuthed his "borrowings" even from the first performance, when, on January 18, 1775, *The Morning Chronicle* traced Lydia back to Steele's Biddy Tipkin (in *The Tender Husband)* and Jack to Cibber's Atall (in *The Double Gallant).*[6] Antecedents claimed over the years for the rivalry intrigues of the play include (1) Ben Jonson's *Everyman in His Humour,* out of whose Stephen, Bobadil, Cob, Matthew, and Brainworm Sheridan ingeniously compounds Bob Acres;[7] (2) Steele's *The Conscious Lovers,* in which, as in *The Rivals,* a father is kept waiting by his son's footman and a son feigns full submission to his father's will;[8] (3) Garrick's *Miss in Her Teens,* in which four rivals contend for the hand of an heiress;[9] (4) Smollett's *Humphry Clinker,* which features a romantic ingenue named Lydia and in which an aunt fancies for herself one of her niece's suitors (cf., Barton and Sir Lucius). Here, too, an extravagant challenge is shamelessly withdrawn (cf., Acres and Tom Eastgate), satisfaction is demanded for unexplained grievances (cf. Sir Lucius vs. Absolute: Jeremy vs. Wilson), and a speech in *Hamlet* suffers malapropriate mangling by an aging aunt (cf., Tabitha Bramble and Mrs. Malaprop).[10]

Prominently cited among sources for the Julia-Faulkland plot, especially as to precedents for Faulkland, are Arthur Murphy's play *All in the Wrong,* William Wycherley's *Love in a Wood,* Matthew Prior's *Nut-Brown Maid,* and Sheridan's mother's novel *The Memoirs of Sidney Bidulph.*[11] In *Sidney Bidulph,* a character named Faulkland confronts his girl friend, after actually killing someone, to exclaim "You see a man whose life is forfeited to the law," just as Sheridan's Faulkland, pretending to manslaughter in testing Julia's loyalty, exclaims to her, "You see before you a wretch, whose life is forfeited."[12] According to Miriam Gabriel and Paul Mueschke, however, only George Colman's play *The Deuce Is in Him* really anticipates poor Faulkland's special psychological dilemma, wherein "The concept of self disassociated from all personal attributes grows into a metaphysical confusion which enmeshes the lover's sense of values."[13]

To Gabriel and Mueschke, Garrick's *Miss in Her Teens* and Colman's *The Deuce Is in Him* seem especially likely sources for *The Rivals,* since they were authored by theater managers whose successes Sheridan hoped to imitate.[14] Perhaps so, but since generalized character types — the testy but affectionate father, the melancholy lover, the capricious heroine, the resourceful serving girl — grace comedy from Plautus on, no debt really stands undisputed, unless it be the characterization of Mrs. Malaprop as enlarged from

Frances Sheridan's unfinished play *A Journey to Bath*, where Mrs. Tryfort speaks of "a progeny of learning" and "contagious countries" and insists that "so much taciturnity doesn't become a young man" — all in the manner of Mrs. Malaprop.[15]

IV   *Mrs. Malaprop*

To be sure, Mrs. Malaprop's literary ancestry reaches back much farther than Frances Sheridan's play. The strain originates no later than Shakespeare's Dogberry and Mrs. Quickly. And certainly Fielding's Slipslop and Smollett's Tabby Bramble adorn the line. In some purely formal senses, all these characters abuse the language precisely as Mrs. Malaprop does. They confuse prefixes (cf., Dogberry's "comprehend" for "apprehend"); they force ridiculous analogies (cf., Mrs. Quickly's "honeysuckle" for "homicidal"); they confuse root syllables (cf. Slipslop's "convicted" for "convinced"); they misapply meanings (cf., Tabbly Bramble's "citation" for "situation").

Yet Mrs. Malaprop distinguishes herself from these kinfolk by the persistence and the sheer range and glory of her word-blunders. She too confuses prefixes ("reprehend" for "comprehend"), forces ridiculous analogies ("pineapple" for "pinnacle"), confuses root syllables ("superfluous" for "superficial"), and misapplies meanings ("progeny" for "prodigy"); but she presses on recklessly, confusing terms similar only in initial syllables ("misanthropy" for "misogynist"), terms similar only in terminal syllables ("perpendicular" for particular"), terms identical in root but tellingly different in suffix ("artifice" for "artistry"), terms identical in initial and terminal syllables but different in medial roots ("perpetrated" for "perfected"), terms similar but for interchanged letters ("felicity" for "facility"), terms identical but for prefix ("incomprehensible" for "comprehensible"). Moreover, she is mightily given to words neither appropriate to their contexts nor redolent of words that are ("simony," "fluxions," "hydrostatics").

The splendid urbanity of Mrs. Malaprop's blunders and their driving deliberateness separate her still farther from her forebears. Slipslop's shabby pronunciations, her "delemy" for "dilemma," "ironing" for "irony," and "confidous" for "confident," could never corrupt Mrs. Malaprop's tongue, nor could Tabby's crude spelling her pen. No homely Dogberry-like innocence redeems her pretensions. And, since multisyllabic Latinate words are her passion (and her undoing), she could never mistake the splendid Latin pronoun "horum" for the disgusting Anglo-Saxon word "whore," as Mrs. Quickly does in *The Merry Wives of Windsor*.

In their contexts, Mrs. Malaprop's blunders everywhere outrage expectations — hence their comic force. Sometimes she simply says the opposite of what she means: "Lucy — if ever you betray what you are intrusted with . . . you forfeit my malevolence for ever" (I, 2, p. 41). But usually she thrusts her audience into a wildly inept frame of reference, an unexpected domain of thought. Perhaps a concrete association supplants a properly abstract one: "He is the very Pineapple of politeness!" (III, 3, p. 68) — or vice versa: "she's as headstrong as an allegory on the banks of Nile" (III, 3, p. 73). Perhaps the new association carries an aptness unsuspected by Mrs. Malaprop: "Caparisons don't become a young woman" (IV, 2, p. 83), or perhaps it insults her grandly: "*Yours, while meretricious, Delia*" (II, 2, p. 57). Occasionally the new association deflates the rhetoric: "You have no more feeling than one of the Derbyshire Putrefactions" (V, 1, p. 102). Sometimes it inflates it: "it is the use of my oracular tongue" (III, 3, p. 69); but usually it shifts the auditor not up or down but out. He delights less in the innuendo than in the ineptness. For malaprorisms rarely generate significant double meaning; they rather attack meaning and destroy it altogether. The context stifles the new associations, and the whole utterance simply collapses into nonsense.

Although malapropisms — some seventy of them throughout the play — dominate Mrs. Malaprop's speech, they hold their comic force because of their splendid variety and because she usually delivers them with commanding authority and in flawless syntax. Virtually as much wonder, then, attaches to the fineness of her phrases as to the word blunders punctuating them. And, since she is curiously inconsistent, now using words accurately and now not, expectations continually suffer shock; the comic effect consistently takes hold. From the added awareness, moreover, that Mrs. Malaprop can sometimes speak sensibly emerges a new dimension of comedy — that ridiculing her affectations. To be sure, her most astonishing malapropisms ornament her consultative tones, in the discourse on female education, for example (I, 2, p. 39), where her most studied pretensions appear. But so settled is her vanity that malapropisms even invade her highest expressions of passion, as when she fears for Sir Lucius' life. They even invade her private reflections, as when she plots to remove Lydia from her "intuition."

In short, her language betrays a character tainted in every quality of mind and feeling by extravagant affectations.

These affectations chiefly show themselves in her pretensions to learning and youth. More significantly, however, they emphasize telling lapses in her humanity. Although her own appetites are lively enough, and virtually undisciplined, she expects Lydia to resign without question all proper human claim to *"preference"* and *"aversion"* (I, 2, p. 38). Memory and affection are to her mere mechanical operations, to be switched on and off as self-interest demands (I, 2, p. 38). Other people serve merely as pawns to her selfishness, and she disallows personal integrity in others. Her own personality is a contrived sham, a fraud so confirmed by practice as to infect every motive and action, every thought and utterance. And, since she takes appearances for realities, deceiving no one more fully than herself, she falls instant prey to flattery. *"I am told,"* writes Ensign Beverley to Lydia, *"that the same ridiculous vanity, which makes her dress up her coarse features, and deck her dull chat with hard words which she don't understand . . . does also lay her open to the grossest deceptions from flattery and pretended admiration* (III, 3, p. 69).

What must be emphasized at last is that the comic range of her language — the property perhaps separating the malapropism from all other kinds of comic word blunder — comprehends every nuance of her character. On the simplest level, her blunders seem innocent folly. But their relentlessness, their authority, the frictions they strike against all surrounding rhetoric, the infection they plant within all her states of mind, all her feelings — all these effects define the greater depths and subtleties of her vanity. And, as speech after speech collapses into nonsense, Sheridan and these speeches reopen the moral void from which Mrs. Malaprop's affectations arise.

V Language and Characterization

Certainly Mrs. Malaprop's provocative language supports J. Q. Adams's view that "the life of the play is in the dialogue."[16] Otto Reinert even holds that "The play is a masterpiece if for no other reason than that it is a feat — or feast — of language."[17] But to most critics — including Adams and Reinert — the brilliant language of *The Rivals* is a mixed blessing. The characters, says Adams, talk not to each other but to the audience; and Reinert concedes that the several comic modes informing the play — its language among them — exact a price in "significant unity."[18] According to G. H. Nettleton, Sheridan's sparkling dialogue in this and other plays supplants depth of expression, serving best to portray "the manners of society rather than the springs of human character."[19] And Allan Rodway sees the dialogue as obstructing character development. The characters "start off as possible beings," he says, but "they do not evolve or display unexpected facets, so as to become as rounded as the requirements of plot might allow."[20]

Actually, all these representative twentieth-century views are eloquently and summarily anticipated by John Jeffrey, who in 1826, writing for the *Edinburgh Review,* complained of "too few indications of noble or serious passion" in *The Rivals,* and he remarked of the language that "the good things are all detached and finished, and independent each in itself."[21] Certainly Jeffrey and the others are right about the divisive effects of language in *The Rivals.* As George Niederauer has recently argued, three distinct traditions of comic language — the traditions of wit, humor, and sentiment — assert themselves rather independently in the play.[22] And, actually, the distinctions pointed by language are yet sharper than Niederauer indicates; for language in *The Rivals* everywhere signals specific characterization. The auditor's ear tags each voice it hears — Fag's polished quips, Jack's cadenced phrases, Lydia's lyric hyperboles, Mrs. Malaprop's "derangment of epitaphs" — and thus the madrigal works out its resolution, its voices distinct and dissonant to the final chord.

To say that language in *The Rivals* everywhere signals characterization is to suggest that language betokens the personal qualities of the speakers. Just as Mrs. Malaprop's word-blunders symbolize the moral vacuity of her character, so Bob Acres' referential oaths expose his fatuous efforts to disguise his rural background. They clearly indicate, as George Niederauer puts it, "the impossibility of the fellow from Clod Hall ever becoming a member of the elite, on an equal footing with Captain Absolute."[23] The function of language as a key to character in *The Rivals* causes Allan Rodway to see Sheridan's people less as the "humour" characters Louis Kronenberger and others see them to be than as wit characters who reveal their absurdity through speech rather than through action.[24] In fact, they seem a curious blending of the wit and "humour" traditions — certainly not wit characters in the stricter Restoration sense, wherein the psychological interplay of fancy and imagination determines qualities of speech and social acceptability, and not "humour" characters in the stricter Jonsonian sense, wherein a ruling passion dominates every private motive. Yet the characters clearly evince marked "humour"-like dispositions, and clearly their language reflects their relative social acceptability. As Jean Dulck and Ashley Thorndike observe, however, nowhere in *The Rivals* do curiosities of language or fixed dispositions completely eclipse individuality,[25] not even in the characterization of Sir Lucius O'Trigger, who conforms in many ways to the stock stage Irishman of the 1770's.[26]

Since most of the characters in *The Rivals* are simple and predictable, critics worry about the ambiguous characterizations of Julia and Faulkland. One time-worn view sees Sheridan as intending these characters as sops to the sentimentalists — and many members of the first-night audience really did take them quite seriously.[27] Another widely held view, one strongest pressed by Rose Snider, regards them as satiric butts who reinforce the general anti-sentimentalism of the play.[28] Rightly enough, Arthur Sherbo recalls that Sheridan did not "divulge his intention in writing the mawkish scenes between Julia and Faulkland." The "vexed question" posed by these characters, says Sherbo, possibly "does not admit of solution."[29] But, as this chapter attests more fully below, the most logical answer to the Julia-Faulkland dilemma must see Julia as a major thematic touchstone for the play, not as a comic or satiric butt (despite her flights of sentimental rhetoric) and Faulkland as a sympathetic fool, played so as to generate "a comic sense of the character's failings," to use Leigh Hunt's words.[30] The play nowhere condemns Faulkland's earnest devotion to Julia — or hers to him. It does not satirize heartfelt passion. It rather laughs, quite mildly and good naturedly, at the subtle emotional confusion in which a man "not feeling why he should be lov'd . . . suspects that he is not lov'd enough" (I, 2, p. 35).

VI *Structure and Theme*

In commenting on the structure of *The Rivals*, critics usually see Julia as a foil for Lydia and Jack as a foil for Faulkland; but they complain that the two love plots are not closely enough related. The actions are too unlike, says Niederauer, and "there is no parallel struggle, intrigue, or deception."[31] Writing in 1906, G. H. Nettleton observed that the Julia-Faulkland business is "so poorly linked with the main plot that it is well-nigh excised from acting versions of *The Rivals*";[32] then he describes in an appendix Joseph Jefferson's acting version, showing how easily Julia's part is omitted entirely and Faulkland's curtailed to a single scene, the encounter with Bob Acres (II, 1).[33]

In addition to the "main plot of comical romance" and "a secondary plot in serio-romantic counterpoint," Otto Reinert isolates two "subsidiary plotlets," the Sir Lucius-"Delia" correspondence and the duel intrigues. All four actions, he holds, are but loosely joined, as the play "pursues its merry and casual way of wit and speech and situation."[34] To Sailendra Kumar Sen, this casualness is a structural catastrophe. After Act III, scene 1, he says, the play is "so busy with Acres, Sir Lucius, Faulkland, and Julia that only now and then can it spare time for Lydia and Absolute." "People who should matter less to the play appropriate the bigger share of action. The resolution of the principal action proceeds very slowly and with many interruptions; and, in spite of a succession of amusing situations and the brilliant dialogue, the reader tires and feels that *The Rivals,* even in its present version, is a long play."[35]

Although usually displeased by the casual interplay of plot strains in *The Rivals,* critics often like the brisk intrigue of the principal action. Granting the basic Absolute-Beverley deception, they say, none of the complications really wrenches probability. And the intrigue generates one hilarious comic irony after another: in Lydia's failure to recognize Beverley as Jack, in Mrs. Malaprop's ushering Beverley into Lydia's presence, in Jack's being forced to marry the very girl he intends to elope with, and in the most crushing irony of all — that the girl who wanted Jack when her aunt forbade him rejects him when the aunt assents. Quite perceptively, Otto Reinert identifies the recognition scene, when Lydia discovers Jack's true identity, as "the comical equivalent of true Aristotelian *anagnorisis.*" In this scene, says Reinert, "The title of the play assumes its subtlest meaning as the Captain realizes that he is his own most dangerous rival."[36]

But, to most readers, the main plot lacks serious meaning, just as the subplot lacks honesty and depth. The whole play, writes Aubrey De Selincourt, "is a bubble — a nothing."[37] Seeking to patch together some thematic salvage, critics note that the play does expose the absurdity of dueling; that by parodying Falstaff's speech on honor in *Henry IV* (Part I), it attacks the folly of dueling, dramatizing through the character of Sir Lucius the dehumanizing effects of the dueling code.[38] Furthermore, it exposes with splendid comic insight the outrage of eighteenth-century marriage customs, where parental tyranny rules the choice of a mate and where wealth and high birth count for everything.[39]

Most importantly to several critics, *The Rivals* satirizes sentimental comedy. According to Rose Snider, Sheridan satirizes through Lydia "that harmless but ridiculous phase of sentimentality consisting in an excessive revelry in the romantic."[40] Through Julia, he satirizes a second and especially distasteful phase of sentimentality — the "exaggerated promenading of one's [own] virtues." Commenting that Sheridan "uses the Restoration comic method of ridiculing the folly of offenses against a code — in this case the code of common sense," George Niederauer sees the playwright taking "the excesses of the sentimental tradition" as his chief target of satire.[41] But, like H. T. E. Perry, like Reinert, and like most other careful critics of the play, Niederauer acknowledges an uncertainty in Sheridan's satiric posture, in that Julia's characterization seems more sympathetic than not, and in that the Julia-Faulkland conflict seems partially serious, or serio-comic.[42] Realistic critics have to admit, then, that, while dramatic history celebrates *The Rivals* as a laughing comedy, a comedy fashioned to combat the sentimental mode, its case against sentimentality is inconclusive.

All told, the play presents troubled critical credentials. Honest criticism must see (1) that the language of *The Rivals* has divisive effects, that it obstructs every casual colloquy among characters, that it obtrudes itself as language, offering sometimes to reduce characterization to caricature; (2) that the "humour"-like dispositions of the characters promote yet further divisiveness, crippling character development, robbing characters of individuality; (3) that the primary and secondary plots are but loosely joined and that the later stage business devotes prominent space to the antics of subordinate characters; (4) that themes, assuming there are any, are vaguely defined and inconsistently dramatized. Readers expecting highly unified Classical comedy in *The Rivals* inevitably suffer disappointment, as do those expecting hard-driving satire against sentimentalism.

But, when freed from the narrow formal conventions usually imposed upon it and from the demands of a preconceived satiric burden, the play asserts a formal logic and a thematic substance overlooked even by its most enthusiastic admirers. Since the key to its form and substance may very well lie in Sheridan's unfinished little treatise on female education, his "Royal Sanctuary," it is proper in what remains of this chapter to analyze the play in relation to the treatise, perhaps to resolve some apparent failings in *The Rivals* and to answer some of the major critical complaints against it.

VII   *Form and Meaning*

No one knows just when Sheridan wrote the "Royal Sanctuary," but its place among his papers suggests a date between 1769, when he rejoined his family after leaving Harrow, and 1774, when he wrote *The Rivals*. Cecil Price (who edits the piece) suggests 1772; Thomas Moore and Fraser Rae favor 1773 or 1774.[43] Walter Sichel and Oscar Sherwin see it as the very "book" mentioned in Sheridan's letter of November 17, 1774, telling Thomas Linley that *The Rivals* is "within a few days" of rehearsal.[44] "I have been very seriously at work on a book, which I am just now sending to the press, and which I think will do me some credit, if it leads to nothing else."[45]

Whether or not the "Sanctuary" is that book, it closely resembles the epilogue to *The Rivals*, an epilogue firmly attributed to the playwright and claiming in its second line to state the "*Moral*" of the play. The play shows, it says, that "Man's social happiness" rests wholly with woman; that men of every station yield to woman's influence, adoring her beauty. In the penultimate stanza, it complains that too few men avail themselves of woman's wit and judgment, the "lasting charms" which fix beauty's darts. Then, in conclusion, it argues that, if woman's good sense properly prevailed, man would need no other school. Honoring her grace and intelligence, "Our Beaux" would be "Sham'd into sense," achieving wisdom through proper practices of gallantry. To improve their homage to her, in short, they would gladly light "The Lamp of Knowledge at the Torch of Love."[46]

In effect, the epilogue simply versifies the presiding premises of the "Sanctuary": Women "have and ever have had" an "unaccountable influence over us" (51).[47] The "incense of our Love and respect for them, creates the Atmosphere of our Souls, which corrects and melio[r]ates the beams of Knowledge" (49). "Were the Minds of all Women cultivated by inspiration, man would become wise of course" (51). Were women but refined by instruction, "each silly Macaroni" would blush to enter their company (58). Men would then consider it fashionable to be "wise and virtuous, to be brave and honourable," for "Love would be their Object, their Guardian, their Instructor. Love would give them wisdom, Genius and honour" (58). In the words of the epilogue, they "Would gladly light, their homage to improve,/ The Lamp of Knowledge at the Torch of Love."

The whole argument of the "Sanctuary" runs as follows: (1) to promote virtue one should promote woman's welfare; (2) God placed woman above man's jurisdiction; she serves to polish man's nature; (3) some "unachal [?] wits"[48] consider woman naturally subservient, but the cultures which most enslave her are themselves the most brutish; (4) since woman is made of man's rib, not of mere clay, she is substantially superior to him; she is more beautiful of form and spirit; and man's inclination — despite his supposed superiority — is to worship her, obeying even vice in her; (5) since woman wields a prevailing spiritual influence over man, man should worship her next to God, giving every attention to her happiness and improvement; (6) to promote the highest charity, then, the Queen should establish a "Royal Sanctuary," an academy providing young women of gentle birth protection from all eventualities of poverty or neglect and instructing them in practical basic studies — practical sciences, history, dancing, embroidery, music, poetry, drawing, riding, and home economics — all the while assuring them the guidance of a clergyman of uncommon character, who would perhaps catechize them in the precepts of *The Whole Duty of Man;* the instruction should omit classical languages and "Novels that show Human Nature depraved"; (7) if established, such a sanctuary would encourage comparable institutions among tradespeople; it would also promise ladies constant refuge from need, cause men to study to deserve their wives (thus generating a "religious love"), reduce foppery among men who prey on woman's ignorance, and promote wisdom and virtue.

This whole rhapsodic discourse reflects a high romantic earnestness. Very seriously, if a bit sophomorically, the young projector assesses the human condition, explaining in a grand cosmic way — encompassing cultural history since Adam's rib — the most basic and persistent of all human conflicts — the fiercely ironic battle of the sexes. Despite an uncontrollable subservience to woman, the piece concludes, man doggedly enforces ignorance upon her, proudly exercising the advantages of his physical superiority. And a world thus ruled by ill-educated women is a hopeless miasma of vice, stupidity, and folly.

Since the central argument of the "Royal Sanctuary" is identical to the self-declared "moral" of *The Rivals,* as defined by its epilogue, the little treatise certainly assists a reading of the play. In fact, several quite specific details of character and situation suggest that *The Rivals* is — at least in part — a comic rendering of the "Royal Sanctuary." In the "Royal Sanctuary," for example, people who enslave women and enforce ignorance upon them are said to be brutish and unreasonable, depraved in knowledge, virtue, and politeness (49). Reasonableness naturally furthers respect for women, respect which "is a Plant that thrives in the Sun of

Knowledge, and in proportion as we cheer its beams, it flourishes and repays us with its fruits" (49). But people who cut themselves off from reason tend to oppress women. They are like the Turks, whose sexual attachments are merely appetitive and whose eyes blink "against the beams of Learning" (50).

Sir Anthony Absolute is just such a one. Unreasonable, appetitive, and brutish, he contrives to keep women absolutely illiterate, looking upon them as mere livestock on the estate (II, 1, p. 53). But from the days of his daring elopement with Jack's mother to his patient petition for Lydia's hand, his whole life attests an irony boldly argued by the "Royal Sanctuary": the indomitable influence of women, even over male supremacists. Certainly his fierce anti-feminism just emboldens Lydia Languish's brand of defiant folly; and, in arguing against female education, he even comes off worse than his adversary, Mrs. Malaprop, several of whose ideas (e.g. the study of home economics and geography) seem drawn straight from the "Royal Sanctuary." Both the play and the treatise damn his un-enlightened attitude to female education, even while they credit his suspicions of novels and lending libraries.

Just as Sir Anthony recalls the rude anti-feminist of the "Royal Sanctuary," so Lydia seems its ill-educated female. Although the treatise approves study of Arcadian romances, it emphatically denounces most novels, branding them figures of "depraved and Corrupted Society" (55). Thus, by reading novels damned by con-temporary critics as "too luxuriant for the eye of delicacy" or "beyond the reach of probability," Lydia seriously miseducates herself, as she probably does in defiling *The Whole Duty of Man*.[49] In failing, furthermore, to perceive "that there are other Passions in Man than Love" ("Sanctuary," 55), she shows herself deficient in history — a major subject in the curriculum of the academy. As an ill-educated female, moreover, she is at once the object of man's adoration and the instrument of his torment, just as the "Royal Sanctuary" warns.

The characters of the ill-educated heroine and the unenlightened father, then, reveal deficiencies specifically denounced by the "Royal Sanctuary." And in yet more general ways, especially as regards the main intrigue, the great social ironies deplored by the treatise define the comic ironies dramatized in the play. The world of the play, like the world of the treatise, is dominated by women: Lydia, Mrs. Malaprop, Lucy, Julia. And the conflicts ring comic variations on the ironies of female dominion. Quite unlike his father,

Jack Absolute intimates in his first interview with Mrs. Malaprop that he admires "unaffected learning" in women (III, 3, p. 67). He is a sensible and practical young man; and the main thrust of the comedy comes of this practical young man's efforts to achieve sensible aims in an utterly illogical world. With splendid patience he accommodates his will to everyone else's persistent folly: to Lucy's duplicity, to Sir Lucius' bellicosity, to Sir Anthony's tyranny, to Lydia's caprice. But despite his goodnaturedness, despite his willingness to wait out the effects of other people's whimsy, the whirling vortex of folly finally sucks him in and offers to get him killed. The play emphasizes that Lydia's caprice chiefly endangers Jack at last; for his frustration at suffering her whimsical rebuff — when she clearly loves him and when no external barrier obstructs their union — renders him incompetent to deal sensibly with the challenges of Acres and Sir Lucius. The crowning irony of Jack's experience is that he must be a fool to shock Lydia from her folly: first posing as Mr. Saunderson (V, 2, p. 102), then presenting himself in two identities on the duel field. She realizes just in time that irresponsible caprice can aggravate life-and-death conflicts. Poor Jack perceives her folly all along but can only wish she were reasonably sensible, for by the nature of his manhood — as the "Royal Sanctuary" would interpret it — he is compelled, despite her folly, to "love even guilt in her" (51).

Read in the light of the "Royal Sanctuary," the Jack Absolute-Lydia Languish intrigues take on significant social dimensions. They dramatize the confusions plaguing mankind since the Fall — perhaps even before it — confusions consequent upon man's effort to accommodate to woman's irrevocable influence. Since Sir Anthony's solution, keeping woman ignorant, is unthinkably barbarous (and goes as clearly counter to the sympathies of the comedy as to the argument of the treatise), it is best to educate women to sensible judgment, thus to promote social harmony. At the close of the play, of course, Lydia openly acknowledges her earlier dangerous caprice. She sees that, by exercising sensible judgment, she could have cemented harmony long before, probably preventing the foolishness at King's Mead-Fields.

The "Royal Sanctuary" also suggests a likely reading of the Julia-Faulkland business, especially in regard to Sheridan's intentions for Julia. In the context of the "Royal Sanctuary," Julia seems not an object of ridicule but an authentic portrait of Sheridan's ideal woman. Although the play does not mention her academic training,

it does indicate, through Bob Acres, her mastery of major accomplishments recommended for the curriculum of the "Royal
Sanctuary" (56): singing, dancing, concertizing. In every way,
moreover, she reflects the high womanly virtues defined in the
treatise, such virtues as prudence, sympathy, loyalty. Eager to fulfill
her role as a loving helpmate, she promises to assist Faulkland
through every adversity, to reform his temper with "persevering
attention" and "unreproaching kindness," to gain a "dearer influence" over him (V, 1, p. 98). She demonstrates the beauty, grace,
and divinity of soul created, according to the "Royal Sanctuary," to
refine mankind.

And the rhetoric of her devotion, even her speech about virtuous
love with a Cherub's hand smoothing the brow of upbraiding
thought and plucking the thorn from compunction (V, 1, p. 96),
perfectly complements in style the ecstatic apotheosis of
womanhood in the treatise. With women, it says, "th[e] enthusiasm
of Poetry, and the Idolatry of Love is the simple voice of Nature,
they were *meant* to polish our nature, we should be Brutes without
them. They are our Angels, our Mistresses, our Souls" (48). From
man's rib God molded a form "more beautiful, more graceful, more
divine," breathing into it a soul "more beautiful, more graceful,
more divine" (51). Certainly Julia's character nowhere exaggerates
these effusions. Against them, she is not a satiric butt. In a sense,
furthermore, the "Royal Sanctuary" explains her extraordinary
gratitude to Faulkland for saving her life — a mere instinctive act in
Lydia's view — for woman's physical survival, says the little treatise,
very often depends upon man's brutal strength. Julia's womanly virtue cannot alone save her life (54).

Just possibly, the "Royal Sanctuary" even helps resolve
Faulkland's enigmatic character. If Sir Anthony's masculine tyranny
and Lydia's ill-schooled judgment confuse social harmony, so do
Faulkland's nagging doubts about Julia's loyalty and about his own
personal worth. And, if Sir Anthony and Lydia suffer flawed education, so does Faulkland. As Jean Dulck suggests, he is Thomas
Sheridan's ill-educated Englishman: unstable, hesitant, self-
reproving.[50] Julia considers him "too proud, too noble, to be jealous"
(I, 2, p. 35); and tradition has it that Sheridan thought this "The
only Speech in the Play that cannot be omitted!"[51] But, proud and
noble as he is, his curious psychological malady blinds him to the
"influencing power of Virtue" in virtuous women (again to use
words from the "Royal Sanctuary," 52). In Julia, he possesses the

brightest star in the ascendant — open, honest, above pretense, above caprice — but his folly, the erratic vacillations of vanity and diffidence, forbids his trusting her and almost causes him to lose her. When at the end of the play she takes him back quite against her better judgment, it is proper to hope that his basic nobility will attune him at last to the power of her virtue.

When read in the light of the "Royal Sanctuary," *The Rivals* obviously gathers structural and thematic strength. Structurally, it presents Jack and Julia as the centers of two actions, one featuring the whole man — practical, sensible, solid — the other the whole woman — gracious, lyric, sensitive. The remaining characters, their peculiarities heightened by tricks of language and "humour"-like whims and passions, suggest the partial views of life with which the whole man and the whole woman must cope. Since these views must amply dramatize themselves, the better to point a comprehensive range of human experience within the play, they cannot be said to constitute a minor action. Furthermore, the duel intrigues thought by Sen to overwhelm the later action of the play properly anticipate the splendid comic resolution on King's Mead-Fields, where the loose and casual action of the early scenes achieves a tight dramatic intensity. Much of the overall comic effect of *The Rivals* turns, of course, upon the loose interrelationship of plots, the outplay of separate actions leading to a young man's becoming adversary, under an assumed identity, to a friend, then adversary, as himself, to a stranger.

Commenting on the apparent imbalance of the two romance intrigues in *The Rivals*, Ernest Bernbaum points to precedents in "the earliest type of sentimental comedy, in which (as, for example, in Steele's *The Tender Husband*) one of the plots was comic and the other sentimental."[52] Arthur Sherbo recalls such dual plotting in Elizabethan domestic drama but indicates that mid- and late-eighteenth-century plays rarely develop two strikingly disparate plot lines, one serious and one comic. *The Rivals*, he says, is extraordinary in this respect, assuming its secondary plot to be uniformly serious and sentimental.[53]

Very possibly, however, *The Rivals* neither invokes early sentimental conventions nor violates late eighteenth-century ones. Its two large plots are analogues of the same moral exhibit, and the Julia-Faulkland business serves less to contrast with the Jack-Lydia conflicts than to extend them. Both plot lines dramatize obstructions to social harmony — one on a plane of whimsy, of flawed education, of pretense and arbitrary codes of honor; the other on a subtler psychological plane, itself perhaps troubled by flawed education. Ironically, Jack and Julia, who command perception, sensitivity, and general good sense, never exchange a word with one another. And this irony, perhaps more than any other dramatic strategy in the play, defines a presiding theme: the roguery of love.

Jack and Julia are both agents of harmony, but love fixes their affections not upon one another but upon agents of discord. As Fag remarks early in the play, L-O-V-E (he spells it out) causes Jack's dilemma (I, 1, p. 30); and this same love requires Julia at last to deny her resolution and to take Faulkland back (V, 3, p. 112). Precisely according with passages in the "Royal Sanctuary" (54), *The Rivals* shows that life is tempestuous and unpredictable at best, that all are vulnerable to love's roguery. But, like the "Royal Sanctuary," it also suggests that by controlling whimsy and passion, by exercising enlightened good sense, the sexes might at least try to make the world habitable and harmonious for one another.[54]

CHAPTER 5

The Duenna

S T. *Patrick's Day; or the Scheming Lieutenant,* a roistering
farce written by Sheridan for the actor Lawrence Clinch,
appeared at Covent Garden on May 2, 1775, and for five additional
performances before the summer hiatus. Then on November 21,
1775, the Covent Garden Company staged Sheridan's second major
theatrical success, a comic opera called *The Duenna.* Letters written
by the playwright to his father-in-law, who was to supply bits of the
score, indicate how carefully he ordered the songs for his comic
opera, how he adjusted the words to the music and the music to the
situation, even prescribing details of orchestral ornamentation and
fitting melodic qualities to his performers' special vocal talents.
Contemporary periodicals applauded the extraordinary excellence of
the songs; and they also admired the fullness of the characterization,
the intricacies of the intrigue, the musical variety, and the close
marriage of song and situation.[1] Excited theatergoers demanded
seventy-five performances during the 1775 - 76 season and could
have used more, had not the Jew Leoni, in the role of Don Carlos,
required Fridays off to celebrate his faith. In every detail of casting,
libretto, and score, *The Duenna* easily eclipsed all earlier productions of its kind.

This particular kind of musical drama dates to 1762 and the
production of Isaac Bickerstaffe's *Love in a Village,* a cento of songs
composed chiefly by Thomas Arne, with borrowings from George
Frederick Handel, Baldassore Galuppi, Francesco Geminiani,
several English composers, and a couple of traditional Irish airs, all
sifted into the action of a slight and disjointed farce. Bickerstaffe's
work, a "comic opera," represented new artistic departures because
it drew its music from concerted scores rather than ballad melodies,
thus to set itself apart from conventional ballad opera. Actually,
ballad opera had flourished only feebly since 1750. It had birthed at

its zenith, with John Gay's *Beggar's Opera* in 1728, and had fallen at once to decline. After 1750, it was largely supplanted by the Italian burletta, a musical farce featuring recitative dialogue and embellished by Italian ballad airs. And with the English burletta *Midas*, produced in January, 1764, Kane O'Hara constructed an important link between ballad and comic operas in English; for he adapted both ballad and concerted songs to his piece. By 1761, formal analogues for English comic opera had also emerged in the French *comédie à ariette*, just as *comédie en vaudeville* had earlier anticipated English ballad opera. And so rapidly did comic opera develop in England that by 1768 such playwrights as Bickerstaffe were designing libretti for original and homogeneous scores. But Sheridan perfected the form by sharpening characterization and tightening plot, and he fashioned the best singing roles for the best singers, the best acting roles for the best actors.[2]

I *The Play*

The Duenna compounds many stock ingredients of comic intrigue (the tyrannical father, the rebellious daughter, the impoverished suitor) and many stock devices (multiple disguises, humiliating discoveries, intricately complex situations). In it, the beautiful young Donna Louisa escapes from her father's house to avoid marrying a repulsive, fortune-seeking Jew named Isaac Mendoza. She leaves home disguised as her duenna, Margaret; and Margaret in turn poses as Louisa, purposing to woo Mendoza for herself. In a second intrigue, Louisa's friend Donna Clara flees from her own father's house to escape what she calls the "insolent importunities" of Louisa's brother Ferdinand and the "selfish violence" of her stepmother, who intends to rob her of her inheritance by sending her into a convent. Once on their own, the two girls exchange identities; and Isaac, aided by his friend Don Carlos, consequently assists Louisa to a rendezvous with his own rival, Antonio. In comparable confusions, Isaac agrees to elope with Margaret, thinking he elopes with Louisa; Don Jerome (Louisa's father) blesses her marriage to Antonio, thinking she is marrying Mendoza; and Ferdinand renounces his friendship with Antonio, thinking him a rival for Clara. But the proper couples are at last married by a Falstaff-like priest, Father Paul, whom they discover at his debaucheries in the priory. And Isaac Mendoza, realizing he has married the Duenna, leaves for Jerusalem hotly pursued by his bride.

Source hunters cite many antecedents to these little intrigues.

Like Dryden's *The Spanish Fryar,* for example, Sheridan's play lampoons debauched clergymen; and, like Wycherley's *The Country Wife,* it puts girls into boys' clothing to confuse and embarrass the men. Like Mrs. Centlivre's *The Wonder,* it claims an Iberian setting, has one heroine exchange identities with another, lodges one of them in a convent to escape some masculine insolence; and, like Molière's *Le Sicilien,* it opens with a valet's soulful lamentations against his master's taxing nightlife. Of course, nothing definitely attests Sheridan's debt to these plays; for, as with *The Rivals,* analogous comic conventions hardly define debts. In fact, Sheridan's own recent experience of love rivalries, elopements, and convents supplied in themselves comic situations enough.[3] If literary sources there be, however, none seems more likely than his own mother's prose tale of *Eugenia and Adelaide* with its disguise complications, its convent episodes, its duenna, its Clara and Ferdinand, its garden rendezvous, its concluding double marriage. It, too, is set in Spain; but, like *The Duenna,* as Jean Dulck remarks, it generates an atmosphere more vaguely Mediterranean than Spanish. Local color plays no authentic part in either piece.[4]

But, by removing his action from familiar English surroundings, Sheridan sharpens the conventionality of his play. Quite deliberately and self-consciously, he manipulates the stock strategies of comedy, wringing hilarity from them and building through them what one clever critic calls an "unstable equilibrium between poetry and parody." At one moment "we are laughing at the self-conscious sparkle of the dialogue or the skilful mechanism of the plot," while at the next "we are touched and charmed by the real beauty of the lyrics."[5] Through this "unstable equilibrium," Sheridan heightens the hilarity of his conventional situations while yet pointing the serious values informing them.

Of course, many of these values are themselves conventional to comedy. They emphasize the superior moral worth of individual freedom, especially freedom of mind and will, in its struggles against arbitrary counter-authority. Quite conventionally, youth is aligned with freedom; age, with authority. Innocent young love is pitted as usual against ruthless parental will. But subtler obstructionist forces thicken the conflict. In Clara's rejection of Ferdinand, for example, ill-reasoned scruples challenge the impulses of love, just as Ferdinand's suspicions of Antonio find love-anxiety challenging good judgment. Like Faulkland before them, then, Clara and Ferdinand allow personal psychological conflicts to encumber their freedom.

The priory scene, furthermore, significantly broadens the conflict of
freedom versus authority, serving not merely to satirize Roman
Catholicism, not merely to inflate bourgeois Protestant egos, but also
to represent the powerfully organized and highly corruptible institutions everywhere threatening private freedom. It is not Father
Paul's self-indulgence that offends in the priory scene; it is his
hypocrisy, the thought that he should label his debaucheries
devotions, that he should accept bribes even as he denounces them,
that he should use the prestige of his institution to enrich himself,
even while debasing other people's virtues and wills. Roman
Catholic actors and theater managers understandably dislike the
roles of Father Paul and his colleagues; indeed, the earliest Italian
versions of the play excise the parts.[6] But the fleshly antics of the
jolly friars certainly toughen the moral fabric of the play. Together
with the flawed scruples of Clara and the stupid absolutism of Don
Jerome, these antics form a complex of barriers to constructive personal will, a complex ranging from innocent misapprehensions
(easily enough corrected by private resolve) to massive institutional
tyranny (virtually beyond correction). And, since the obstructionist
forces in the play aggravate all the intrigues in it (the flights, deceits,
and disguises), the intrigues in turn give formal definition to the
hopeless stupidity of the obstructionist forces themselves.

If serious values jostle the comic intrigues of the play, they also
reinforce the ironies always plaguing the obstructing characters —
certainly some of the best comic ironies in Sheridan's canon. While
old Margaret waits within, for example, Don Jerome prepares Mendoza to meet Louisa, for whom Margaret has substituted herself. To
whet Mendoza's appetite for the girl, Don Jerome presents himself
as the model and source of her beauty and boasts absolute authority
over her. Thus at the expense of his own stupid vanity, he heaps
irony after irony upon himself, preparing for the moment when
Mendoza must see in dreadful fact the shocking crone so ex-
travagantly represented to him as Louisa. The scene achieves at least
six levels of irony, levels built upon the audience's awareness (1) that
Jerome's boast of authority is an empty boast, since Louisa has
flagrantly disobeyed him; (2) that the woman described as waiting
within is indeed Margaret, not Louisa; (3) that, while Jerome fancies
himself the pattern of Louisa's beauty, he really resembles old
Margaret; (4) that, in high anticipation of meeting Louisa, Mendoza
must actually meet the old bearded crone; (5) that Margaret's
resemblance to Jerome just ratifies Mendoza's assumption that she is

his daughter; (6) that Jerome's vanity in offering himself as the source and model of Louisa's beauty just redoubles, rather than reduces, his moral and physical grotesqueness. Of course, when Mendoza actually meets Margaret, the play's thickening ironies also gather around him, as he gulps down his disgust for her, woos her, even elopes with her merely to gratify his avarice. And all these ironies, however cruel, engage the audience's sense of ethical rightness, foreshadowing the time when the obstructing agents, though temporarily successful in tethering freedom and youth, must answer to justice and good sense.

Ironies also condition the dialogue of *The Duenna*. Critics rightly enough complain that the play fails to show "recondite wit" and "quaint fancy," two qualities seen by Brander Matthews as heightening the brilliance of *The School for Scandal*.[7] To show that the dialogue "rather plays than shines," Moore cites a metaphor comparing serenaders to Egyptian embalmers who practice "extracting the brain thro' the ears" (I, 2, p. 194). The playwright mistakes "labored conceits for fancies," says Moore.[8] And it is certainly true that some of the similitudes collapse under their own weight: "nobility without an estate is as ridiculous as gold-lace on a frize-coat" (I, 3, p. 215); "love, like a cradled infant, is lull'd by a sad melody" (I, 1, p. 188). But similitudes in *The Duenna* carry very little weight. The comic force of the language derives rather from innuendos relating to the play's action, innuendos both issuing from and adding to the delightful situational ironies. "But when I saw you," says Margaret to Mendoza, "I was never more struck in my life." "That was just my case too, madam; I was struck all on a heap for my part" (II, 2, p. 210). "O Sir, you have the most insinuating manner," she says later, "but indeed you shou'd get rid of that odious beard — one might as well kiss an hedge-hog." "Yes ma'am," he replies; (aside) "the razor wou'dn't be amiss for either of us" (II, 2, p. 211). Quite typically for the play, the associational properties of language enliven and deepen the comedy; and, since the characters and situations are little suited to recondite wit, *The Duenna* suffers little for the want of it.

Walter Sichel cleverly remarks that *The Duenna* "moves even where it does not breathe";[9] and, indeed, it gives life to only four characters: Margaret, Jerome, Father Paul, and Mendoza; but all of them really remain largely caricature. The young lovers are mostly bland types; and Don Carlos, an excrescence, is included to sing an occasional pretty song. Except in the case of Margaret, whose individuality originates in external grotesquerie, characterization in the best-realized characters derives from ironies indicting their folly. Like situation and dialogue, then, characterization roots itself in comic irony. Father Paul, for example, gains important new dimensions of folly when he damns for a glutton a simple porter who tries to drain the friar's own empty wine glass. Similarly, Jerome's role as absolutist fool gains depth and complexity through his rejoicing in Clara's father's misfortunes ("an old fool! imposed on by a girl") while ironically describing his own character and situation.

And these same kinds of ironies — though more puckishly imagined — set Mendoza off as the best-drawn character in the play. As he brings Antonio to rendezvous with the real Louisa, whom he thinks to be Donna Clara, he delights in his own sinister resourcefulness, rejoicing in his "little cunning head" and repeatedly styling himself "a Machiavel, a very Machiavel" (II, 4, p. 221). In fact, he is a "comic Machiavel"; the phrase perfectly suits him. He is Christopher Marlowe's Barabas turned inside out, exciting through his selfish cunning as much roistering comedy as Barabas excites tragedy. In splendid Machiavellian spirit — open, direct, frankly treacherous — he charts his own humiliation. And the comic irony informing his role as Machiavel is that same which binds *The Duenna* in situation, language, and characterization into a tight conceptual whole.

II   *The Music*

Although the elder Thomas Linley, Sheridan's father-in-law, generally receives credit for scoring *The Duenna*, recent scholarship indicates that his son, the younger Thomas, did most of the work. Young Tom apparently composed eight of the thirty-one musical pieces, including the intricate overture and the lively finale to Act I; and Linley Senior probably composed four of them. At least seven are popular Scots or Irish melodies (principally Scots); two are the work of William Jackson of Exeter; and two are not determined as to source. Four British composers — John Ernest Galliard, Michael Arne, William Hayes, and Thomas Morley — each composed one piece, as did four Italian composers — Geminiani, Giordani, Rauzzini, and Sacchini.[10] Musically, then, the opera is very much a pastiche; but enough of the music was written to order, after Sheridan's specifications and by the two Linleys, to sustain artistic integrity.

The elder Linley's reasons for passing the job on to young Tom must remain at least partially conjectural. Roger Fiske, who has traced the origins of most of the tunes in the opera, suggests that Linley disliked the plot of the play (assuming he knew it) and perhaps identified himself with Don Jerome, the dupe of a disobedient daughter.[11] But better reasons appear in a letter dated September 28, 1775, from Linley to Garrick: Linley explains that he disapproves of the whole practice of "compiling" operas from available tunes. Proper procedure dictates, he feels, that the score be written expressly for the libretto and that the completed libretto be always before the composer since "No musician can set a song properly unless he understands the character, — and knows the performer who is to exhibit it." He also indicates that he will not identify his own name or his son's with the opera and that he will help Sheridan only because he knows he needs the money, although certainly "nature will not permit" him to be indifferent to Sheridan's success.[12] Linley's reluctance to offer significant help and his apparent failure to do so suggest, then, that Sheridan himself bore virtually independent responsibility both for the libretto of *The Duenna* and for the songs selected (or commissioned) to score it. Possibly, too, Sheridan's judgment more strongly asserted itself upon young Tom than it could have done upon Thomas Senior. Consequently, the playwright's taste even touched details of orchestration and tonal coloring.

Sheridan designed the libretto for five voices: coloratura (Clara), soprano (Louisa), mezzo (Margaret), tenor (Antonio, Ferdinand, and Don Carlos), and baritone (Don Jerome and Isaac Mendoza). Apparently only two members of the original cast — Leoni, in the role of Don Carlos, and Miss Brown, in the role of Clara — really sang exceptionally well;[13] so, in writing their parts, he gave them relatively more to sing than to speak and act. The distribution of musical numbers, including duets and trios, runs as follows: Antonio, seven; Carlos, five; Ferdinand, seven; Isaac, four; Clara, six; Louisa, eight; Margaret, one; Friars, one. Of the thirty-one numbers, ten are ensembles (quintet, one; glees with chorus, two; duet, three; trio, four); twenty-one are airs. Sheridan's awareness of the problems of production raised by each of these pieces appears in the valuable series of letters that he wrote to his father-in-law during October and November, 1775, outlining his plans and needs.

The first letter, chiefly imploring Linley to assist in staging the third act ensembles, presents few insights into Sheridan's designs for the opera; but it does imply that he has sifted certain of Linley's

"proposed alterations," weighing them against his own plans and
against the tastes and expectations of the London theater audience.[14]
The second letter, however, tactfully specifies the music needed to
close Act I. This point in the action finds Mendoza hurrying to Don
Jerome's house, and he intends to leave Louisa (whom he thinks to
be Clara) protected by Don Carlos in his own lodgings and to send
Antonio to her there. Already, then, the situation is thick with irony,
even as Isaac rushes on toward ever greater follies. And, since it is
important that the finale both catch the irony of the situation and
display Leoni's voice to best advantage, Sheridan calls for a three-
part setting: a duet sung by Isaac and Louisa, followed by an air
sung by Carlos, and concluding with a trio sung by the three of
them. The first part is a dialogue in which Isaac explains to Louisa
that he must get along to his mistress; and Louisa in turn wishes him
good fortune in his wooing. For this part, Sheridan orders "a pert,
sprightly air," hoping to promote through incongruities of word and
music a mock earnestness in the attitudes of both Isaac and Louisa
— since Isaac really cares little for Louisa's welfare and Louisa
knows that Isaac is hurrying into old Margaret's snare. "They are
neither of them in earnest in what they say," Sheridan writes. In the
second part, however, Leoni "takes it up seriously," the better to
show off his own voice. Sheridan therefore orders Leoni's kind of
song: "in a plaintive or pastoral style," with light accompaniment
and ample opportunity to make cadences, for "he never gets so
much applause as when he makes a cadence." In recovering the
comic zest of the action, the young playwright asks finally that the
third part renew the pert sprightliness of the first. Thus he anticipates in theory all the artistic and pragmatic demands of his
finale; and, since one of the Linley's (probably young Tom) obliged
him with every ingredient of his musical recipe, he achieved in fact
the dramatic effects he sought.[15]

In writing about *The Beggar's Opera*, Allardyce Nicoll remarks
the special delight surely enjoyed by contemporary audiences as
they listened to fresh words sung to well-known tunes, tunes already
carrying distinct associations for them. Sheridan's third letter to
Linley, October 23 - 27 (?), shows him shaping his own opera to this
same special delight: he insists that the friars at their wine sing new
words to well-known tunes. "The joke will be much less," he writes,
"for these jolly fathers to sing anything new, than to give what the
audience are used to annex the idea of jollity to." In this third letter,
he also lays plans for a lively glee to be sung by Isaac, Antonio, and

Father Paul as "in great raptures" Isaac and Antonio drag the fat
priest off to marry them. Obviously, however, he is groping for apt
new words to replace those usually sung to "Dr. Harrington's
catch," the tune tentatively selected for the piece. He considers —
"for a stage effect" — having Paul sing a bass pattern under the
baritone and tenor of the two other voices; but, for some reason, the
whole scheme is abandoned; the piece is not used. Quite to good
effect, however, he uses two passionate songs prescribed in this
letter: Ferdinand's "Sharp is the woe" (III, 2), "a broken, passionate
affair," which opens with an emotional recitative, and Clara's
"Adieu, thou dreary pile" (III, 3), a coloratura showpiece featuring
obbligato dialogues between voice and oboe. Anticipating the flashy
musical requirements of this piece, Sheridan carefully worked the
phrase "sullen echo" into his words: "I have lugged in 'Echo,' who is
always allowed to play her part." Thus he opened generous opportunities for the intricate oboe echoes gracing the finished score.[16]
And thus he demonstrated again quite clearly that music and libretto
in *The Duenna* are not separate conceptual units but are both lively
products of his own mind and art.

It is worthwhile adding here that Sheridan's revisions of the
autograph version of the text — revisions recorded by Moore and
Sichel[17] — also attest to the thorough control he exercised over his
materials. He curtailed the opening speech; he deleted two
superfluous stanzas from the song "Give Isaac the nymph" (II, 1); he
removed two unnecessary characters, a Don Pedro, who figured as
Clara's cousin, and a maid named Lisetta; he omitted a cumbersome
duet in Act II, scene 2, but added such important songs as "What
bard, O time discover" (II, 4) and "When sable night" (I, 5). He
suppressed the charming lyric "I ne'er could any lustre see" (I, 2),
then reinstated it. All the revisions show his shaping and tightening
of the whole piece by accelerating action, sharpening dialogue, ad-
justing proportions, lopping off excrescences, and refining the interplay of music and speech. These changes reflect the practical
good judgment necessary to artistic and theatrical success.

III *Words and Music*

Certainly the interplay of music and speech defines the best excellence of *The Duenna*. The music never annihilates character or
action — as is so often the case in comic opera — but always
amplifies them in various important ways. The gentle air "When
sable night," for example, both lyricizes the exposition and opens

valuable insights into character and motive. In it, Clara recalls the previous night when she had ejected Ferdinand from her room. His own spoken account of the episode pictures her in high moral pother. But her song, its melody hinting a restive passion, indicates that she had feigned prudery merely to conceal (and control) erotic impulses. The song perfectly dramatizes her motives, furnishing insights not readily evoked by speech.

Similar extensions of feeling appear in Ferdinand's song "Could I her faults remember," in which he deplores the supremacy of passion over reason, and in Louisa's "What bard, O time discover," in which she endures a dispiriting "interval of expectation" while waiting for Antonio. Other musical numbers have the effect of extending and lyricizing the dialogue (Antonio's "I ne'er could any lustre see" and "Friendship is the bond of reason"). Yet others establish comic situations ("Give Isaac the nymph") or define relationships (Finale to Act I), or enrich atmosphere ("Adieu, thou dreary pile"), or heighten the rhetoric of dispute ("Believe me good Sir"). A few of the songs are closely tailored to the situations stimulating theme (Clara's "By him we love offended"). But most of them encompass the particular in the general; they develop maxims or lyric experiences at once applicable to the play's action and to the common lot of man. Such songs, of course, carry much of the thematic burden of the play by furnishing general observations on such matters as parental authority, the psychology of love, crabbed age and youth, jealousy, friendship — matters commenting upon the dramatic action of the play.

Dulck notes that the songs point the structural outlines of *The Duenna*, that they terminate every act, virtually every scene, summarizing the action and enriching its effects.[18] One of the pivotal recognition scenes, moreover — Ferdinand's recognition of Clara and Louisa (III, 6) — unfolds in song, attesting the close marriage of music and action. Nothing attests this marriage more fully, however, than the sharp comic ironies pointed by the songs. When Don Carlos sings his exaggerated compliment to Isaac and Margaret — "Ah! sure a pair was never seen,/So justly fram'd to meet by nature" — he engages ironies comparable to those shaping the characterization, conflict, and dialogue; and he demonstrates that *The Duenna* is very much of a piece. True enough, as a recent critic writes, the libretto "stands on its own feet as a brilliant stage play";[19] but it really has no integrity apart from the music. Through emotive reaches that extend from puckish frivolity to warm lyric tenderness, the music breathes a subtle, complex vitality into the themes of the play, engaging for the action important responses of mind and heart. From the fusion of words and music, then, emerges a comedy of great substance, delicacy, and force — one perhaps not illogically thought by William Hazlitt to be "a perfect work of art."[20]

CHAPTER 6

The School for Scandal

S HERIDAN announced *The School for Scandal* well before
he finished writing it, and holographs of the last five
scenes show great signs of haste. Earlier scenes went through
numerous transcripts, all copied into notebooks; but these final ones
were drafted only once on detached sheets of paper, the last sheet
bearing that "curious specimen of doxology," as Moore calls it, the
now famous jotting "—— finis —— Thank God! RBS," under which
appeared the prompter's antiphon, also in Sheridan's hand, "Amen!
W. Hopkins."[1] The hasty completion of *The School for Scandal*
belies, however, the long years of its evolution. No one knows just
when Sheridan started developing the play. Sichel suggests 1772.[2]
Quite obviously, in any case, two fragmentary comedies anticipate
it: the "Teazle-play" and the "Clerimont-play," both of them yet
extant in various stages of development.

I   *The Teazle-Play*

In its earliest form the "Teazle-play" seems designed for a two-act
afterpiece, though a five-act outline suggests itself in later expan-
sions and revisions. The entire surviving text, consisting of two long
scenes, is clearly experimental, reflecting without interruption or
comment the playwright's developing concepts of character and
scene. At the outset of the opening fragment, for example, Old
Solomon Teazle identifies himself as thrice wed and as an "old
widower" recently retired from trade and now remarried to a
fashionable woman thirty years his junior; but, by the end of the
scene, he is Sir Peter Teazle, an old bachelor only recently married to
an extravagant country wife. At the outset, "Old Solomon Teazle"
addresses himself in soliloquy. His steward Jarvis next joins him to
discuss Mrs. Teazle's extravagances. Then "Lady" Teazle suddenly
emerges in the scene, quite unannounced and obviously as an

94

afterthought. Just as uncermoniously, Jarvis now disappears; and a colloquy between "Sir Peter" Teazle and his bride concludes the episode. As the scene develops, then, it reaches always toward the form finally given it in *The School for Scandal,* the delightful domestic quarrel opening Act II.

The second fragment of the "Teazle-play" features Young Pliant — originally Young Plausible — receiving Lady Teazle in his bachelor quarters. Here the dialogue, which finally contributes to the famous "screen scene" (Act IV, scene 3 of the finished play), suggests two major conflicts designed for the "Teazle-play": the continuing friction between the Teazles, and an intrigue of some kind between Lady Teazle and Young Pliant. Other characters cited in a tentative *dramatis personae* suggest yet a third complication, an attachment between Young Pliant's brother (originally listed as Captain Harry Plausible) and a certain Maria, variously identified in the manuscript as Lady Teazle's niece and her daughter-in-law. With but minor refinements, all these conflicts figure at last in *The School for Scandal;* and yet others evolve through the fragmentary "Clerimont-play."

II *The Clerimont-Play*

Sheridan apparently intended the "Clerimont-play" to be a farce or a two-act comedy. It turns upon the efforts of Lady Sneerwell, a scandalmongering vixen, to alienate the affections of her ward Maria from the hero Clerimont, for whom she nurtures her own secret affection; and she works her stratagems through forged letters and newspaper scandals. The earliest shadowings of this comedy appear in some disjointed scraps of dialogue labeled by Sheridan *"The Slanderers — A Pump-Room Scene,"* jottings possibly done as early as 1772, though more likely done in 1774 after Sheridan read, as Crompton Rhodes surmises, a scandal story in *The Town and Country Magazine,* a story closely paralleling the proposed plot of the "Clerimont-play."[3] Possibly earlier than the "Clerimont-play" comes also a rough scenario setting out the same Sneerwell action but calling the romantic principals Florival and Emma, rather than Clerimont and Maria.

Sheridan roughed three quite full fragments for the "Clerimont-play." The first puts Lady Sneerwell in intimate conference with Spatter, the slander-journalist, as she describes to him her past distresses and her current affections and arranges through him to separate Clerimont and Maria. The second finds Maria complaining to Lady Sneerwell about Clerimont's increasing coolness to her; it also introduces old Mrs. Candour, a crone notorious for killing reputations by defending them. The third fragment, a long and involved one, finds Clerimont accusing Sir Benjamin Backbite of eloping with his sister, who has run away from her uncle's house in the country. It also places Sir Benjamin and Maria in a conversation that is contrived by Lady Sneerwell to be discovered by Clerimont; then it closes with Clerimont's lamentations over Maria's apparent infidelity to him, lamentations mouthed to Lady Sneerwell while she plays ombre with Sir Christopher Crab. Not a trace of this third fragment finds its way into *The School for Scandal.* The first one, however, contributes generously to the early parts of Act I, scene 1; and the second furnishes bits of dialogue for later portions of that same scene.

III   *The Fragments Combined*

In the "Teazle-play" and "Clerimont-play," then, Sheridan forged most of the characters he was to use in *The School for Scandal;* and he defined many of the situations and sentiments. As Rhodes suggests, the idea to combine the two fragments probably emerged with the conception of the scandal college. In developing this concept, Sheridan installed Lady Sneerwell as president of the college, leaving her original character largely unchanged; then he staffed her faculty with characters from the "Clerimont-play." He transferred Mrs. Candour to the new play intact; but he reduced Sir Benjamin Backbite from an active villain to a fatuous fop, and he remolded Sir Christopher Crab into Crabtree. Spatter, the scandalmonger of the opening scene, he renamed Miss Verjuice for the penultimate version of the amalgam; then he gave the role to Snake, who already figured in the fifth act of that version.

Needing then a novitiate for the college, he brought in Lady Teazle, whom he refined from the coarse third wife of old Solomon into a bright and naturally civilized young country matron. And with her came all the retinue of the Teazle play: Sir Peter Teazle, at once victim and caustic critic of the scandal college; Joseph Surface, the hypocritical moralist (originally Young Pliant); and Charles Surface, the amiable protagonist (originally Frank Pliant). Suggested by both the contributing fragments, Maria fitted comfortably into the new play, still nebulously connected to the Teazle family and still intended by Lady Sneerwell to be her dupe. Only the steward Jarvis and the priggish Sir Charles Clerimont found no place in the finished product. Moore had seen Clerimont as "the embryo of Charles Surface,"[4] but Rhodes is right in insisting that Charles develops from the young spendthrift of the "Teazle-play."[5]

Rhodes also suggests that the inspiration for the scandal college might have come from the gossip club the Collegiates in Jonson's *Epicoene*, a play featuring a character named Clerimont. George Colman had adapted Jonson's comedy in 1776 and had written a prologue for it paraphrased in the *Town and Country Magazine* as comparing "the College Ladies in the days of Ben Jonson to the Coterie of the present *ton*."[6] Other sources of inspiration might have included, as Jean Dulck suggests, an article in *The Gentleman's Magazine* for February, 1735, one using the phrase "School for Scandal."[7] And of course several plays of the 1760's and 1770's used the phrase "School for" in their titles: *The School for Lovers, The School for Wives, The School for Rakes*, etc.

But, whatever the inspiration, it yet remained for Sheridan, after establishing the scandal college and combining the two fragmentary plays, to compose the greatest moments of his comedy: Sir Oliver Surface's appearances as Little Premium and Mr. Stanley, the picture auction scene, the screen scene — all the strategies of deceit and embarrassment informing the play. A play about Lady Sneerwell and her scandal college, it is also a play about the Teazles, an old bachelor and his unbroken filly of a wife. But, centrally, the play is about two brothers, Joseph and Charles Surface, and about the disposition of their Uncle Oliver's fortune — how in the interest of money Joseph seeks the affections of Sir Peter's ward Maria, who loves Charles; how in the interest of pleasure he offers to debauch Sir Peter's wife, naming Charles in the intrigue; how, counseled by the old retainer, Rowley, Sir Oliver tests his nephews' fidelity and finds Joseph sadly wanting.

In the final version, Lady Sneerwell arranges through her wily associate, Snake, to defame the generous scapegrace Charles Surface, with whom she is herself secretly in love. Her plan is to wreck Charles's character in the eyes of Maria, the wealthy young ward of Sir Peter Teazle, and thereby to free Charles for herself while freeing Maria for Joseph Surface, who wants Maria's money. Gaming and carousing have already so tainted Charles's reputation that Sir Peter quite gives him up, preferring instead the calculating hypocrite, Joseph, whose fabricated morality thoroughly abuses Sir Peter's credulousness. In fact, only old Rowley, a faithful retainer of the Surface family, steadfastly champions Charles; and, when Sir Oliver

Surface, the uncle of Charles and Joseph, returns to England after a sixteen-year residence in India, Rowley encourages him to assume disguises for the purpose of testing his nephews' characters.

Disguised, then, as the Christian moneylender, Mr. Premium, Sir Oliver first visits Charles in his lodgings where he finds his nephew busy at hazard with a company of roisterers. So desperately does he need money that, when asked for collateral, he first offers security against the life of his Uncle Oliver, from whom he claims great expectations; and he then proceeds carelessly to put the family canvases on auction, blithely "knocking down" his ancestors at whatever price Sir Oliver will pay. Prospects darken for Charles until Sir Oliver's own picture reaches the block; then the auction stops, for Charles steadfastly refuses to sell his uncle's picture, even when offered for it the sum of all the others combined. "Little Noll," he says, has always been more than generous to him; and filial devotion forbids his selling the picture. He thus secures himself in Sir Oliver's good favor and proceeds immediately to other acts of kindness by sending to an indigent relative, Mr. Stanley, a large portion of the money paid him for the pictures.

In the role of Mr. Stanley, Sir Oliver presents himself later to the hypocritical Joseph; but, before this unfortunate encounter, Joseph manages to ruin himself completely in the esteem of Sir Peter Teazle, whose approval he has needed in his designs upon Maria. Under the tutelage of a ruthless scandal cabal (including Sir Benjamin Backbite, Mr. Crabtree, Mrs. Candour, Joseph Surface, and Lady Sneerwell), Sir Peter's bright young country wife has begun to affect city ways, both by indulging in wild extravagances (to her husbands's great distress) and by acceding quite tentatively to Joseph Surface's offer to be her beau. She sits in Joseph's library one day, listening unconvinced to his arguments against good reputation, when Sir Peter suddenly drops in, an awkward surprise which sends her scurrying behind a screen.

Thinking himself alone with Joseph, Sir Peter candidly unfolds his domestic troubles. He indicates his decision to provide Lady Teazle a separate maintenance because she seems to despise him and because the gossip is that she favors Charles Surface. At just this moment, Charles is announced; and Sir Peter, exacting from Joseph a promise to question Charles about Lady Teazle, starts to hide behind the screen. He actually sees Lady Teazle's skirts there; but Joseph, after sheepishly identifying the lady as a little French milliner from the neighborhood, a lady hiding to preserve what reputation she yet has to lose, desperately steers him into a closet to avoid his recognizing his wife. Joseph dutifully questions Charles about Lady Teazle; but, when Charles makes comments touching Joseph's own involvement with the lady, Joseph quickly chokes the colloquy by revealing Sir Peter's presence. Charles immediately hales Sir Peter forth; and, as he listens to the old gentleman's apologies, a servant whispers the arrival of yet another caller, Lady Sneerwell, whom Joseph chooses to receive below. While he is out of the room, Sir Peter, who is still much delighted to think of the "moral" Joseph's liaison with a French milliner, tells Charles about the lady behind the screen. Of course, Charles must immediately have her out; and, just as Joseph re-enters, the screen falls to reveal the mortified Lady Teazle.

Joseph's star has sunk, but the humiliations of this ignominy promote no charity in him. When Sir Oliver visits him in the role of Mr. Stanley, he rejects the poor fellow with lies about his own financial distress. Now clearly known for what he is, Joseph forfeits Sir Oliver's good will, even as he had earlier forfeited Sir Peter's. Lady Teazle reforms and is forgiven; Maria accepts Charles's proposal of marriage (and his assurances of reformation); and Lady Sneerwell, enraged by disappointed hopes, must stew at last in her own frustrated malice.

In constructing his play Sheridan combined several thematic conventions: the scandal cabal, the country wife, the old bachelor, the two brothers, the male Cinderella. That such discrete conventions could blend themselves into a distinctive and highly successful comedy attests to Sheridan's lively literary perception. And the smashing success of *The School for Scandal* attests to his impeccable theatrical sense, not only because the play features dazzling theatrical business in the auction scene, the screen scene, and in the Mr. Stanley scene, but also because the first Drury Lane cast actually shaped the characterization.

Discussing "The Original Cast of *The School for Scandal*,"[8] Christian Deelman demonstrates quite convincingly that Sheridan designed his characters after the best talents, sometimes even after the actual personalities, of his cast. Consequently, John Palmer fell naturally into his role as Joseph Surface, just as "Gentleman" Smith fell into his as Charles. And, in playing Trip, the enterprising gentleman's gentleman, Philip La Mash needed only to play himself. From all reports, Mrs. Abington was a perfect Lady Teazle, of whose sharp delivery Thomas King, her equally effective Sir Peter, recalled that "every word stabbed." Only Maria, as played by

Priscilla Hopkins, was a disappointment. The role was originally intended for "Perdita" Robinson, whose pregnancy prevented her
playing it; and Moore writes that Sheridan declined to bring Charles
and Maria together before the final scene because he could not trust
the actors in these roles with a love scene.[9] However, *The School for
Scandal* was never better acted than on its opening night at Drury
Lane on May 8, 1777.

IV   The School *and the Critics*

Modern criticism sees the sustained success of *The School for
Scandal* as a largely theatrical phenomenon, one promoted by scin-
tillating dialogue, memorable caricatures, and brilliant situations;
but, as penetrating and coherent literature, the play claims few
champions. It "teaches no lesson and points no distinctive moral,"
writes Ashley Thorndike.[10] Louis Kronenberger complains that
Sheridan's "sense of the theatre wins out in the end over his
knowledge of the world." To his "sharp and emphatic dramaturgy,"
Kroneberger insists, Sheridan attaches only "mild and sanctified"
subject matter; he indulges the "generally acceptable"; he inveighs
"only against what is demonstrably safe." The play "clicks its heels
before conventional morality."[11] According to Cleanth Brooks and
Robert Heilman, this obeisance to conventional morality leads
Sheridan at last to emphasize "what is admirable, what is 'virtuous,'
rather than keeping our attention upon what is ridiculous." In
rewarding virtue with money, moreover, he reduces to triviality the
play's major assessment of human values.[12]

Some critics complain that Sheridan's failure to engage subtle
moral issues results in, and from, the shallow and deceptive
characterizations in *The School for Scandal*. To Henry James, Joseph
Surface "is a mere walking gentleman who stands for hypocrisy and
is labeled in very large letters."[13] George Niederauer sees Charles as
"a weak, passive, vacuous younger son, who consistently permits the
decisions and plans of others to break upon him like waves."[14]
Prosser Hall Frye argues that Joseph is really no worse than
Charles;[15] Andrew Schiller insists that Charles is indeed no better
than Joseph.[16] Brooks and Heilman resolve the issue by suggesting
that "Joseph's 'good' side is entirely imaginary, and Charles's 'bad'
side is insignificant." The complexity of the Surface brothers, they
say, is "somewhat synthetic."[17] Only Lady Teazle wins universal
critical acclaim; as Hazlitt puts it, her character is subtly com-
pounded "of artificial refinement and natural vivacity."[18] But, by

boldly eclipsing Maria, she overshadows the proper heroine of the play and disturbs the structural balance.

And structure aggravates another critical sore spot: critical unrest centers on the fusion of the two fragments. Restating an opening night complaint, Andrew Schiller argues that the scandal plot seems almost "entirely separable from the main structure of the action." Despite the importance given it by the title, he writes, "it is the most awkward thing in the play."[19] Brooks Atkinson objects to the unfortunate shift in tone apparent between the second and third acts when the scandal wit yields to the comedy of sentiment and situation.[20] And J. R. de J. Jackson, developing a point earlier hinted by Sichel, suggests that, in joining the two fragments, Sheridan scrupulously salvaged the witty aphorisms he had coined for the separate plays.[21] To preserve an aphorism, then, he sometimes transferred whole pieces of dialogue from one character to another, promoting inconsistencies in characterization and betraying a readiness to sacrifice plot and character for witty dialogue.

Of all the strictures brought against *The School for Scandal*, those indicting the scandal scenes as structural excrescences remain the easiest to answer. Just fifty years after the first performance, Moore labeled these complaints "hypercritical."[22] As Schiller properly indicates, the screen scene clearly links the scandal plot to the other leading intrigues in the play.[23] And in a more general way, as G. H. Nettleton long ago noted, the scandal characters furnish a necessary background for Lady Teazle's indiscretions.[24] They also generate the atmosphere necessary to control the play's sentimentality; and they justify Sir Oliver's deceptions in testing his nephews, since a world diseased by scandalmongering does not support open inquiry.

Strictures against theme and characterization are harder to answer. Apart from the satire against scandal journalism and a thrust or two against usury and the sale of annuities to minors, the play seems indeed to avoid moral confrontation and to champion bland good nature rather than ridiculing hypocrisy. The characters do lack the ambivalence usually apparent in superior characterization. Nevertheless, the play dazzles audiences — in the study perhaps even more than the theater — with its complexities and its intricate tissue of ironies, details of action, dialogue, and characterization obviously devised to control and deepen the final sentimental statement. Many charges brought against *The School for Scandal*, even those indicting the mismanagement of aphorisms and the moral shallowness in theme and character, lose force when considered against the play's milieu and against the conventions supporting its curious complexities.

V *The Milieu and the Conventions*

Despite old saws to the contrary, *The School for Scandal* does not, of course, restore the Restoration. Sheridan liked to be thought the latter-day Congreve; but, as surely as Congreve's comedy reflects a rationalistic Restoration morality, so Sheridan's reflects the open Christian benevolism of Georgian pulpit theology, the sort of spontaneous charitableness emphasized in R. S. Crane's "Suggestions toward a Genealogy of the 'Man of Feeling'." Eighteenth-century "charity sermons," writes Crane, featured "a long series of amplifications on the theme of man's essential 'good nature,'" picturing the human being as "naturally disposed to impulses of pity and benevolence."[25] As a man of feeling himself, and one certainly tuned to the moral scruples of his audience, Sheridan declined to compromise the religious doctrine of good nature. He therefore struck a comic posture remarkably capable of exposing folly while reaffirming basic human benevolence.

In his doctoral essay "The Laughing Comedy of the Eighteenth Century," David A. Nelson describes some of the techniques used by Sheridan to strike this subtle comic posture.[26] Recalling that the surface brilliance of the play often blinds critics to the major sources of comedy in it, Nelson traces these sources to comic situations involving disguised persons, mistaken identities, hiding scenes, discovery scenes: five such situations as opposed to only two episodes drawing comedy from satire or witty dialogue. From the days of Farquhar, Nelson remarks, wit had gradually declined in English comedy because it could not flourish apart from malice; and Sheridan manages wit successfully in *The School for Scandal* by introducing only a few marginally malicious characters into it. The good-natured people show no great flair for wit, and the comedy rises mainly from situations building to comic embarrassments. Embarrassment provides the comic *dynamis* for the play, both in the episodes centering upon Joseph Surface and on Charles. Quite conventionally to laughing comedy, then — here as in Goldsmith's *She Stoops to Conquer* and in *The Rivals* — laughter results from a comic *anagnorisis* in which the character duped ultimately discovers a truth known all along by the audience and all along used by it at his expense.

Also conventional to laughing comedy, according to Nelson, is the illusion of wickedness. The hero-dupes of laughing comedy, even the villains, seem more wicked than indeed they are, a circumstance really necessary to the doctrine of human benevolence, which considers wickedness an unnatural moral condition. If *The School for Scandal* generates the illusion of wickedness, however, it does not therefore minimize the brooding threat of evil. Louis Kronenberger writes that "The play is concerned with the *imputation* of sinning," that "of sin itself there is absolutely nothing."[27] But while, as he suggests, the screen scene turns on circumstantial evidence and while Joseph is a villain without really showing himself a rake, the intent of treachery is clear in him, just as Lady Teazle seriously considers cuckolding Sir Peter; and, of course, Joseph actually commits the grievous sin of uncharity. Evil in *The School for Scandal* is dangerously imminent, as the characters engage in practices certain to corrupt their essential good natures.

If Sheridan's comic posture in *The School for Scandal* relates to the doctrine of Christian benevolence, it properly shows evil as an acquisition of discipline and art. Professor Crane quotes one charity sermon as arguing that, while "Nature inclines us to Humanity, yet Custom and bad Principles may give us another *Bias*, and make us unconcerned what others feel. But Nature, without Art and Force used upon it, seldom proves cruel." Another sermon holds that "A Man must be disciplined to hardness of Heart, and neild into Cruelty." And yet another, taking the positive view, insists that "when we see any of our Fellow-Creatures in Circumstances of Distress, we are naturally, I had almost said, mechanically inclined to be helpful to them. . . . When men follow Nature in those tender Motions of it, which incline them to Acts of Kindness and Charity, they will not be easy, except they lay hold of the proper Occasion of exerting them."[28]

The ethical position of *The School for Scandal* accords perfectly with these sermons. Charity and basic human benevolence relate themselves in the play to spontaneity, directness, simplicity. Malice and uncharity relate themselves to deviousness, deceit, complexity. As an acquisition of discipline and art, a quality to be learned in the school for scandal, evil implies complex contrivances. Through the conflict between complexity and simplicity, then, Sheridan controls in one dramatic strategy the comic and moral implications of his play.

VI   *The Range of Complexity*

Brooks and Heilman remark that complexity accounts in part for the durability of *The School for Scandal*, that through it Sheridan "combines artistic detachment and moral perception and so avoids the opposite extremes of moralizing on the one hand and indifference on the other."[29] Certainly complexity — conceived as resulting from art or from subtle intellectual contrivances — aligns itself with vice throughout the play. At the very outset, Snake congratulates Lady Sneerwell for the special "delicacy of tint, and mellowness of sneer" distinguishing her scandal. In effect, he admires the art whereby she disciplines herself to vice, her skill in translating simple truth into complex falsehood, simple innocence into complex imputations of treachery. All the stratagems of the scandal college engage such processes of complication, identifying complexity with vice.

Wit in the play, as David Nelson remarks, chiefly serves the ends of malice. Both Sir Peter and Maria insist that true wit really derives from good nature; but the play allows little such good-natured wit. It favors extravagant similitudes born of ill nature and conceived to polish cruelty. Of the marriage of wit and benevolence, Lady Teazle, before reforming, sees the partners as "so near akin that they could never be united"; and Sir Benjamin refines on the figure by supposing them already man and wife "because one seldom sees them together" (II, 2, p. 48).[30] Earlier in the play Lady Sneerwell had argued that the malice of wit is "the barb that makes it stick." And, as if in support of this premise, the complicating force of wit in *The School for Scandal* consistently rallies to the cause of malice, emphasizing the close kinship between complexity and vice.

Complexity accompanies malice in the play in many other ways, of course: in Mrs. Candour's candor, which converts praise to insult; in the marvelous circumstantial lies — those reporting, for example, the screen scene — which sacrifice truth to complex fictive detail; in Joseph Surface's crafty management of sentimental morality, which secures his own hypocrisy; in his larger resourceful management of the whole art of appearances, whereby he seeks the reputation of benevolence "without incurring the expense" (V, I, p. 97). So close at last is the correlation between complexity and evil that complexity, as an agent of evil, assumes an identity apart from the characters generating it. Once set in motion, it threatens everyone it touches, especially the characters who motivate it. Consequently, they perceive, as Joseph does in Act II, that it bears them along by its own force, rendering them the more vulnerable as it races out of control. "Sincerely," says Joseph, "I begin to wish I had never made such a point of gaining so very good a character, for it has led me into so many cursed rogueries that I doubt I shall be exposed at last" (51).

VII *Complexity vs. Simplicity: The Auction Scene and the Screen Scene*

In action preliminary to the auction scene, Charles Surface shows himself a champion of simplicity and directness: "plain dealing in business I always think best," he says to Sir Oliver, whom he believes to be Premium, the Christian moneylender. "Mr. Premium," he had said just before, "the plain state of the matter is this: I am an extravagant young fellow who wants to borrow money" (III, 3, p. 68). Of course, his very directness makes him a comic dupe when he boldly offers Sir Oliver's fortunes in security for his debts, and then puts the family canvases on auction and lets his preferences for practical immediacy quite overwhelm familial tradition. He first opens himself to comic embarrassment when he insists to Premium that Sir Oliver's health sadly suffers from the Indian climate, that now "his nearest relations wouldn't know him" (70). The auction scene promises ever greater embarrassments, each sale heightening Charles's vulnerability. But, in refusing to sell Sir Oliver's picture, he cancels the complications of this brilliant scene; asserts his essential good nature, which he really never compromises; and retains absolute control of events. True enough, his deviousness in misrepresenting Sir Oliver's health will yet embarrass him in Act V when Sir Oliver reveals himself. But the complications threatening to humiliate him in the auction scene cannot assail his simple devotion to his uncle or his basic charitable motives. Here as always, his virtue expresses itself through the uncomplicated immediacy of his conduct. As comic dupe, then, he provokes joyful, sympathetic laughter, but never ridicule.

In striking contrast to the auction scene, the screen scene — which follows hard on it in Act IV — thoroughly humiliates its own dupe, Joseph Surface, and leaves him the apt victim of ridicule. A dramaturgical masterstroke, it transcends the limits of mere comic embarrassment and assumes symbolic importance in the presiding conflict between simplicity and complexity. As Jean Dulck suggests, it is a play within itself, its five acts beginning with Lady Teazle's visit to Joseph's library and concluding with her confession and his disgrace.[31] The servant's interruptions break the first three acts, as he announces first Sir Peter, then Charles, then Lady Sneerwell. The fourth act concludes with the collapse of the screen; and the fifth, a serio-comic resolution to the whole scene, presents the aftermath of the screen's fall, including Charles's discreet withdrawal, Joseph's "explanations," and Lady Teazle's reformation.

The fall of the screen, of course, marks the climax of the scene. Intricate complications precede this climax, and no one of them is more revealing than Joseph's fancy polemics about reputation. He seizes upon Lady Teazle's annoyance at the scandal circulated against her — an annoyance the more frustrating for her own self-conscious innocence — to argue that self-conscious innocence in itself causes her to neglect forms, to "run into a thousand little imprudences," to grow "impatient of Sir Peter's temper, and outrageous at his suspicions." Insisting then that her character is "like a person in a plethora, absolutely dying from too much health" (IV, 3, p. 82), he provokes her famous query: "So, so; then I perceive your prescription is, that I must sin in my own defense, and part with my virtue to preserve my reputation?" Moore writes that, throughout the long development of *The School for Scandal*, Sheridan had kept this splendid quip fresh in his mind.[32] He had jotted it along the margins of his memorandum book, holding it ready for the proper moment; and he could not have found a happier place for it than here at the structural heart of the play. The specious reasoning it displays reflects in turn the ultimate complexity of Joseph's deviousness, a complexity by which vice parades as the primary agent of virtue. Sichel calls Joseph a comic Iago,[33] and the appellation holds especially well in this scene where sound reason yields to intellectual gymnastics. While dazzling and hilarious, Joseph's arguments are also serious and dangerous; for they threaten truth with its own defensive weapons.

With his arguments, of course, Joseph again begets complications he can neither understand nor fully control. He shows clear astonishment at Lady Teazle's interpretation of his logic. And as the screen scene develops, its growing complexities virtually take charge. "A narrow escape, indeed! and a curious situation I'm in, to part man and wife in this manner," Joseph gasps after hiding Lady Teazle behind the screen and her husband in the closet. While the Teazles cooperate in his deceptions, he keeps tentative control of things; but, when Charles appears, the screen of hypocrisy must surely fall. Charles's simple directness will not abide the complex contrivances of Joseph's deceit. The informing conflicts of the screen scene, then, perfectly represent the characters involved in it and their motives: Joseph's hypocrisy and unnatural artifice, Charles's openness and natural spontaneity, Sir Peter's blindness in crediting Joseph's sentiments, and Lady Teazle's pretensions in crediting his arguments. And, on a more comprehensive plane, simple directness, as an agent of virtue in the play, here assails and destroys complexity, as an agent of vice.

After the screen scene, the scandal college bruits the episode abroad, fleshing the bare truth with imaginative circumstantial lies. Joseph and Lady Sneerwell spring their last stratagem, implicating Charles with Lady Sneerwell herself; but their plan is foiled by old Rowley, who pays Snake twice as much to tell the truth as Lady Sneerwell had paid him to lie. Lady Sneerwell storms off, fuming in her disappointment; Joseph follows after to "protect" Charles against her further malice. Sir Peter forgives Lady Teazle; Maria "looks" yes to Charles's proposal of marriage. True benevolence triumphs in every way. At the close, the play declines to pass judgment against anyone; it rather implies that all people are good by nature, even those who cultivate the arts of malice.

The play does not, however, avoid moral issues. Holding that people must discipline themselves to vice, that evil derives from art and industry, it cites the complexities born of vicious industry as the real villains of the piece. These complexities, which outstrip the control even of the people who generate them, do incalculable and indiscriminate damage; and they open no real opportunities for gain. In the case of the scandal college, the play suggests that vice can become habitual, that the arts of malice can gradually stifle basic good nature. Through Lady Teazle's experience, however, it also suggests that, in regaining virtue, one needs only to decline the discipline of vice — in effect, to return one's diploma to the scandal college. From its basic premise of Christian benevolism, then, *The School for Scandal* makes cogent statements about the self-complicating properties of hypocrisy, about false sentiment, malicious candor, wicked insinuation. It exposes the wide-ranging threat of vice even while affirming the ultimate good nature of mankind.[34]

CHAPTER 7

The Critic

IN 1770, Sheridan had collaborated with his friend Nathaniel Brassey Halhed to devise a rehearsal farce, a burlesque burletta called *Ixion*. It featured a playwright-critic named Simile, the embryonic origin of one of Sheridan's finest mature characterizations, Mr. Puff of *The Critic*. With *The Critic*, then, Sheridan brought his career in comedy full circle; for, in important strategies of character and form, his last significant play, itself a rehearsal burlesque, enlarged and perfected his first tentative venture into drama.

At Drury Lane on October 30, 1779, the opening-night audience readily recognized a kinship between *The Critic* and the Duke of Buckingham's still popular *The Rehearsal* (1672). Astute first-nighters might also have sensed kinships nearer home, to some of Fielding's burlesques — *The Author's Farce* (1730), *Eurydice Hiss'd* (1737), *The Historical Register* (1737) — to Garrick's *A Peep Behind the Curtain* (1767), a rehearsal play, and to George Colman's *New Brooms*, a farcical prelude commissioned by Sheridan for performance at Drury Lane on September 21, 1776, the night he assumed management.

Key moments in *The Critic* recall these earlier pieces. In Buckingham's play, for example, major exposition is supposedly spoken offstage outside the hearing of the audience, as in *The Critic;* and saucy actors mangle and excise lines of dialogue as they choose. Fielding's pieces provide burlesque instances of the tearful reunion scene, such as the reunion of the Tomkins family in *The Critic;* and, in the device of the broken sentence, an obliging survivor completes the final sentence of a fallen hero. Fielding also introduces the role of the thinking actor who, like Sheridan's Burleigh in *The Critic*, merely cogitates gravely and says nothing. In *A Peep Behind the Curtain*, Garrick brings members of the Drury Lane staff onto the stage, just as Sheridan does in bringing on the prompter, the carpenter, and the master lamplighter (in the only passage of *The Critic* to be deleted from the authorized edition of 1781). And Colman's *New Brooms* anticipates situations central to the action of *The Critic:* several critics gathered at the home of a colleague to receive aspiring authors and encourage foreign entertainers. Burlesque duels and battles of the sort staged by Sheridan had appeared prominently in theatrical satires by Thomas Duffett and Henry Carey, as well as by Buckingham and Fielding. So quite clearly, as V. C. Clinton-Baddeley remarks, "Sheridan helped himself deliberately to everything of value in the burlesque tradition."[1]

Very much in that tradition he alludes in the play to theatrical and political topics hotly current in 1779. Just a few months earlier, in June, 1779, Spain had declared war on England. At Coxheath near Maidstone the army had established an encampment during the summer to prepare against possible invasion from France. And the combined French and Spanish fleets, now allied in behalf of the American colonies, had appeared in August off Plymouth. The tragedy rehearsed in *The Critic*, so soberly entitled "The Spanish Armada," obviously recalls these grave political events; and no less obvious to contemporary theatergoers were allusions to current theatrical personalities and situations. According to Rhodes, for example, Bannister made his role as Don Whiskerandos in *The Critic* an exaggerated copy of Gentleman Smith's portrayal of Shakespeare's Richard III, just as Miss Pope as Tilburina closely imitated Mrs. Crawford's celebrated mad scenes.[2] Dane Farnsworth Smith sees the original of Sheridan's Dangle as Thomas Vaughan, a self-appointed impresario for the Richmond Theatre;[3] and Sichel sees Whiskerandos as a caricature of the "elegant and haughty" John James Hamilton, late Earl of Abercorn.[4] Puff as theatrical director, according to Sichel, represents John Philip Kemble;[5] and commentators universally agree that Sir Fretful Plagiary represents Richard Cumberland, the sentimental dramatist.

While Puff's "The Spanish Armada" may generally recall Cumberland's *The Battle of Hastings* (1778), allusions to specific plays in *The Critic* are relatively few. To be sure, the scene reuniting the Tomkins family almost certainly echoes a similar scene in John Home's *Douglas*, where Lady Randolph discovers young Norval to be her long lost son. And, in saying that "The stage should be a school of morality," Sheridan's Sneer obviously borrows a line from Hugh Kelly's *False Delicacy*. Sir Fretful once goes outside dramatic literature to steal a line from Charles Churchill's *The Apology*. And scattered allusions to Shakespeare remind first-nighters that *Hamlet* had supplied the mainpiece of the evening.[6] But *The Critic* largely avoids specific parody.

In avoiding specific parody, it distinguishes itself prominently from earlier theatrical burlesque. Buckingham had shot barbs at particular lines in particular contemporary plays, but Sheridan chose rather to parody general literary and theatrical offenses. And, while Buckingham had drawn his playwright-buffoon, Bayes, as a close caricature of John Dryden, Sheridan drew his Puff as a highly individualized free agent, one only occasionally suggesting an actual human model. It is easy to list many other telling differences between *The Critic* and *The Rehearsal* — how Buckingham extended his play into five wearing acts, as against *The Critic's* tight three-act organization; how Buckingham's Bayes presents a tissue of disjointed parodies, while Puff presents a relatively coherent play; how the spectators at Bayes' rehearsal, Johnson and Smith, represent non-theatrical attitudes while Sheridan's Dangle and Sneer are jaded theatrical dilletantes.[7] Telling differences between Sheridan and Fielding just as readily assert themselves, especially in Fielding's complex bookishness and political polemics.[8]

And, when placed alongside Sheridan's obvious borrowings from the burlesque tradition, all these striking differences show him shaping the tradition to his own dramatic aims. What was transmitted to him from Buckingham through Fielding and others, he refurbished and personalized. And through his special kind of general parody and his delightfully individualized characterization, he transcended the limiting particularity of closely topical antecedents. In the process, of course, he enlarged the burlesque tradition itself by rejecting ghosts, oaths, and rhymed couplets because his general target was sentimental tragedy — not the rhymed heroic play. But then he developed burlesque tactics appropriate to his own intent. By having Puff lift a line straight out of *Othello*, for example, he burlesqued the sentimental-tragic vogue of the Shakespearean echo and added a fresh joke to the burlesque granary.[9] He burlesqued the emotive blank verse excesses of sentimental tragedy not by specific parody but by hilarious blank verse excesses of his own, thereby achieving an ingenious double-edged satire leveled both at specific offenses and general artistic follies. In sentimental heroes and heroines lay yet another plum for Sheridan's plucking, and his Tilburina consequently remains, as she was in 1779, an unparalleled study in super-exquisite female sensibility.[10]

In accommodating the burlesque tradition to his own art, Sheridan easily robbed *The Rehearsal* of its supremacy among theatrical burlesques and caused it to seem after 1779 a weak imitation of his own play. And, in embracing *The Critic*, English audiences responded not just to the fresher timeliness of the allegory but also, and perhaps more importantly, to a new complexity in burlesque drama — a play beginning in its opening scenes as provocative satire and moving thereafter into a complex form of burlesque. The play also catches, of course, the amiable spirit of Sheridan's earlier comedy; and it presents several full-blown comic characters, characters no more limited by generic designations, such as "Dangle" and "Sneer" and "Puff," than are Lady Sneerwell and Sir Peter Teazle and Snake in their play.

The Critic features, then, an interplay of three dramatic modes, the comic, the satiric, and the burlesque, with touches additionally of burletta and masque. Through these mixed modes Sheridan neatly frames his indictments of irresponsible criticism, bad theater, fraudulent advertising, and weak art. And he manages in the process to embolden English patriotic spirits. The properties of this interplay best appear in a close analysis of the seven distinct parts of *The Critic*, parts aptly called "sketches" by Dane Farnsworth Smith.[11]

I *Seven Sketches*

The first of these seven sketches presents the self-declared impresario, Mr. Dangle, at breakfast with his wife. They fall at once to heated argument; she attacks his ridiculous passion for the theater; and he insists that "the stage is 'the Mirror of Nature,' " and that actors are the "Abstract, and brief Chronicles of the Time." The conflict between them turns upon one central issue: whether or not idling away one's time in theatrical affairs can be justified during times of national crisis. As Jean Dulck observes, Mrs. Dangle represents stolid English patriotism.[12] When her husband loses patience with newspaper accounts of the French threat, she taxes him with misplaced loyalty, arguing that in times of crisis he should be "at the head of one of the Westminster associations — or trailing a volunteer pike in the Artillery Ground." If the French should invade tomorrow, she adds, his "first enquiry would be, whether they had brought a theatrical troop with them" (195).[13]

And her grievances touch not merely his lack of patriotism: they assail the general smallness of his life. He is "call'd a theatrical Quidnunc, and a mock Maecenas to second-hand authors" (194); he involves himself in the "plague and trouble of theatrical property,

without the profit, or even the credit of the abuse that attends it"
(194); he converts his home into a "register-office for candidate actors, and poets without character" (194). Managers and authors "of
the least merit" merely laugh at his pretensions, realizing that "The
PUBLIC is their CRITIC." In answer, Dangle can only insist that
some credit attaches to providing fiddlers for Lords, securing boxes
for ladies, arranging engagements for actors, and getting answers for
authors. Since the stage is indeed "the Mirror of Nature," he says, a
man of sense can find no better avocation. And certainly there is
"importance in being at the head of a band of critics, who take upon
them to decide for the whole town, whose opinion and patronage all
writers solicit" (195).

Quite obviously this opening episode sets up some forceful comic
indictments. Primarily, it marshals patriotic spirit against theatrical
idling, making irresponsible criticism and all agencies of bad art
causes equal with the French threat for national concern. Danglers,
it implies, are ineffective Englishmen; they are ineffective family
men; they are ineffective human beings. They are as wrongheaded
in their systems of values as in their systems of loyalties. And in indicting them the scene generally flatters the audience, which immediately identifies itself with Mrs. Dangle and rushes with her to
the national defense. It endorses each point of her argument and rejoices above all in that climactic declaration at the close of the scene,
"The PUBLIC is their CRITIC." Thus with force and economy
Sheridan shows that Dangle's folly, though whimsical on the face, is
symptomatic of serious moral and judgmental ills.

In the second of the seven sketches, Mr. Sneer's arrival interrupts
in mid-career the freewheeling domestic squabble of the Dangles,
thrusting the second part of the play into an atmosphere of curious
comic tension, where affected good cheer must mask unsatisfied in-
ner irritations — lest Sneer "hitch" the Dangles into a scandal story
(195). Sneer's sharp-edged sarcasm cuts into everything it meets.
First it slices into Dangle's pretended distaste for his "solicited
solicitations," causing him to admit that he actually likes having a
dozen strangers call on him at breakfast each day, just as he enjoys
receiving fifty letters a week which involve him in other people's affairs (196). Next, and much more subtly, he cuts into Mrs. Dangle's
sensibilities, her preference for pious imitations of the French
comédie larmoyante. "I am quite of your opinion," he agrees; "the
theatre in proper hands, might certainly be made the school of
morality." But then he adds in obvious mock earnestness, "now, I

am sorry to say it, people seem to go there principally for their entertainment!'' (197). Sneer's real attitude toward sentimental comedy
appears in his swipe at the affected scruples of the audience, the
priggishness which allows no *double entendre* or smart innuendo but
insists that Vanbrugh and Congreve undergo a clumsy reformation.
"Yes," he says, "and our prudery in this respect is just on a par with
the artificial bashfulness of a courtezan [*sic*], who encreases the
blush upon her cheek in an exact proportion to the diminution of her
modesty" (197).

Dangle and Sneer both despise spineless sentimental drama, and
they anticipate in this one agreement the partnership they will
finally enter against Mr. Puff's new play. In this second sketch,
however, Sheridan allows them only a whisper of sound judgment.
Immediately after damning bowdlerized comedy, Sneer falls to ad-
miring a new kind of comedy intended to "dramatize the penal laws,
and make the stage a court of ease to the Old Bailey" (197). Thus
neither his judgment nor Dangle's, who shows puzzled interest in
the new scheme, yet stands to be trusted.

In this sketch, Sheridan demonstrates that no character in the
play, not even Mrs. Dangle, speaks consistently for the playwright.
He reserves every privilege of the satirist; and his characters serve as
satiric agents apt at any moment to become satiric butts. In the first
sketch, Mrs. Dangle speaks for the playwright and for every loyal
Englishman; but, in the second, she speaks for herself and falls
directly into folly. Thus Sheridan disengages himself and satirizes
through the erratic tastes of his characters some telling offenses in
playwrights and audiences. As the play proceeds in this complexity,
folly becomes a relative thing: no one is free of it, but some
characters appear more foolish than others; and occasionally a flash
of good sense redeems even the most accomplished fool among
them. Mr. Sneer, furthermore, brings into the play a moral position
now familiar in Sheridan's comedy, that of the urbane confidence
man who, like Snake in *The School for Scandal*, frankly
acknowledges his own roguery and turns it to the service of covert
rogues. "I have brought you two pieces," he says to Dangle, "one of
which you must exert yourself to make the managers accept, I can
tell you that, for 'tis written by a person of consequence" (196).

In the third sketch, Sheridan introduces one of his best-drawn and
most irredeemable fools, Sir Fretful Plagiary. Sir Fretful obviously
caricatures the playwright Richard Cumberland, whose dislike of all
adverse criticism was a generally known fact. During rehearsals of

his *Battle of Hastings* at Drury Lane he had resisted every critical suggestion made by the management. And Sheridan retaliated by dramatizing in *The Critic* an episode probably told him by Garrick and recorded years later in Cumberland's own memoirs, an episode in which Garrick had teased Cumberland by fabricating in his presence a newspaper attack against his famous comedy *The West Indian*.[14] As a comic butt, of course, Sir Fretful easily transcends the limitations of specific caricature and represents at last all the testy and arrogant playwrights who brook no criticism but defend to the end their own indefensible failings.

This time Mrs. Dangle appears as a sentimental plain dealer, a champion of genteel drama who offers to befriend Sir Fretful, even warns him outright that Sneer and Dangle plan to bully him. Dangle in this sketch assumes some of the properties of Mrs. Candour in *The School for Scandal*. He sweetens his venom with persistent declarations of good will, tagging the phrase "though he is my friend" to each stricture he levels at Sir Fretful. And Sneer exploits here as never before his own reputation for double dealing: his two-faced contempt for Sir Fretful ranges from fulsome panegyric to shattering insult. Only Sir Fretful fails to catch the irony in Sneer's praise; and, when Sneer speaks with cruel frankness, the Dangles need only remind Sir Fretful that Sneer never really means what he says.

The sketch organizes itself very much after the lines of Sneer's attack. A brief introduction, played out before Sir Fretful appears, establishes the two critics' true attitude to him: that he is fiercely envious, that he displays an "insidious humility," that his new tragedy is execrable. At his appearance, they gull him with false praise; then, at his own steady insistence, they offer guarded criticisms against his play, citing its lack of incident, its failure to maintain interest, its inordinate length. Since he simply dismisses every complaint, showing himself invulnerable to polite criticism, they finally devise a stratagem in which Sneer fabricates a cruel newspaper attack against him; and here Sneer finds his proper platform. Unable now to disregard the criticism or to charge it to Sneer's double dealing, Sir Fretful can only contrive a hollow laughter and listen to the roll of his offenses: his lack of invention, his lack of taste, his intolerable bombast, his ill-digested tropes, his clumsy imitations of Shakespeare. And in a tempestuous pique he at last flounces off stage, loudly protesting his "calm indifference" to and "philosophic contempt" of all newspaper criticism (205).

After Sir Fretful leaves, his two tormentors congratulate each other for baiting him; they agree, in Sneer's words, that "where a base and personal malignity usurps the place of literary emulation, the aggressor deserves neither quarter nor pity" (205). When Sheridan concludes the sketch by having two arrogant scoundrels mouth moral maxims, he emphasizes that Sir Fretful is the bigger fool for being the dupe of fools and that folly is indeed a complex and relative thing. Of course, the audience clearly perceives the whole range of folly in the scene: it laughs at Sneer and the Dangles as well as at Sir Fretful. And it also laughs at the playwright, who causes Sir Fretful to send his new play to Covent Garden, since the manager of Drury Lane "writes himself." With Sneer and Dangle, however, Sheridan places himself among the less objectionable fools in the sketch. His reputation as an occasional plagiarist, exploited here to good comic effect, pales before the paranoid suspicions of Sir Fretful, who thinks Sheridan capable of using other people's tragic fustian in his own comedies. And, while deriding Sir Fretful's paranoia, the audience possibly finds itself the butt of a subtle joke too; for, in charging Sheridan with plagiarism, Sir Fretful pilfers an image straight out of Charles Churchill's *The Apology*, thereby raising some question as to who the real plagiarist is, Sheridan or Sir Fretful. The question, of course, continues unresolved and leaves the audience laughing at its own confusion.

The fourth sketch provides an interlude between the first major segment of the play, which is climaxed by the disgrace of Sir Fretful, and the second one, which features Mr. Puff and his tragedy. In this segment, Signor Pasticcio Retornello and his three daughters present themselves to Mr. Dangle with the assistance of a French interpreter and on recommendation of two English sponsors, Lady Rondeau and Mrs. Fuge. When they arrive, Mr. Dangle is still busy with Sir Fretful; so Mrs. Dangle receives them into the drawing room. Since the interpreter speaks only a few words of English, he must translate from Italian into French, though he protests that his French rendering is "in English." And poor Mrs. Dangle understands absolutely nothing. Even after her husband appears, the foreigners fail to communicate with anyone since Pasticcio and his interpreter speak simultaneously and too fast. So the company at last gives a pleasant musical audition and withdraws.

However slight this fourth sketch may seem on the face, the comedy in it holds serious implications. Certainly it recalls Dangle's lack of patriotism, his willingness to consort with the enemy merely to ad-

vance his own pretensions. It also recalls Mrs. Dangle's warning that
foreign entertainers might in fact be "foreign emissaries and French
spies . . . disguised like fidlers and figure dancers" (195). Furthermore, it looks forward to the lamentations sent up in Sheridan's
prologue to *The Miniature Picture* (1780) and his epilogue to *The
Fair Circassian* (1781), that foreign entertainers deplete the
resources of the native stage and that support for them betokens dis-
loyalty to the state and to the stage. In all fairness, however,
Sheridan acknowledges through the sketch that foreign entertainments can be diverting. So popular were the French trio and
Italian duet performed here that they were published separately in
1779 and were thus the first part of *The Critic* to see print.[15] According to the issue of 1779, the music was composed by "Signor Geor-
dani," either Tommaso of Naples or his younger brother Giuseppi.
Sheridan possibly supplied the lyrics. And, while he made them
diverting enough, he yet hinted his mistrust of foreign entertainers.
The French trio begins with the declaration, "I have left home to
play my guitar." "Je suis sortis de mon pays pour jouer de ma
Chitarre, qui fait tin, tin, tin," a rather slight reason to leave home,
Sheridan subtly implies.

After Mrs. Dangle leaves with the foreigners to record their addresses and get them refreshments, she never again comes upon the
scene. The introduction of Mr. Puff, then, brings together the three
characters central to the remainder of the play: Puff the amateur
playwright and Dangle and Sneer his critics. This fifth sketch, an exposition of Puff's profession of puffing, adjusts once again the scale
of folly, weighting it decisively in favor of Dangle and Sneer. Of
course, Dangle is still somewhat unpatriotic; Sneer continues as
glibly sarcastic as ever; but Puff surpasses them both in resourceful
roguery. At one point, in fact, Sneer becomes something of a
spokesman for the audience (the charitable part of it anyway), when
he suggests that, by publishing a confession, Puff might warn innocent people against the more insidious kinds of puffing. The distribution of sympathies in this sketch, then, prepares the audience
for the rehearsal sketch to follow in which Dangle and Sneer preside
over Puff's buffoonery.

Like Joseph Surface and Benjamin Backbite before him, however,
Puff is no simple fool: he is brilliant and imaginative in his profession. His extraordinary success at puffing reflects his keen insight
into human nature, from the ill considered outpourings of human
benevolence to the most outrageous displays of human vanity.

Though not wholly devoid of scruples, he concerns himself more with results than motives; and, since as a professional puffer, he must puff himself wherever he can, he gives here a detailed account of his own successes. First, he tells how he came into the profession; how he advertised for handouts while posing in one or another state of wretchedness, as a bankrupt, a burnt out tradesman, a prisoner for debts, a widow with six helpless children. Admitting, however, that these frauds "had always gone rather against" his conscience, he next explains his current and legitimate profession as "scientifically treated" and "reduced to rule." He then presents lively expositions of the puff direct, the puff preliminary, the puff collateral, the puff collusive, the puff oblique or by implication. In all its forms, of course, puffing appeals to pernicious passion, to vanity, jealousy, lust, greed, idle curiosity. Its splendid effectiveness, moreover, signifies the essential shallowness of too many moral and social values, the eagerness with which a society sublimates its worst appetites through brilliant and resourceful advertising. And Puff emphasizes the universal influence of puffing, how it affects the worlds of business, art, and politics. Through him Sheridan demonstrates once again that bad art and bad politics take root in the same soil.

As a basic tactic of the sixth sketch — the "rehearsal" which constitutes Acts II and III of *The Critic* — Sheridan closely interrelates character and situation. Thus Sneer's sarcastic comments on tragedy are characteristically double-edged, implying insult while declaring praise, and Dangle's fulsome solicitousness yet hints ridicule in the name of friendship. D. F. Smith is emphatically right in saying that, as commentators on the rehearsal, these characters show little kinship to Buckingham's Smith and Johnson, who speak in the playwright's voice. Dangle and Sneer everywhere follow their own tastes and mannerisms; and, if the playwright agrees with them, so much the better for him. Similarly, Puff continues very much in character; he does not, as some critics say, dwindle into a mere Bayes. He is not, as others complain, an awkward stand-in for Sir Fretful, who seems to them the apter fool for this sketch.[16] The play rehearsed here is clearly the product of Puff's mind, and it clearly reveals his characteristic turns of thought.

Just as he treats his profession scientifically and reduces it to rule, so he composes his play by rules and conventions. At the outset, for example, he establishes the controlling maxim (altering Shakespeare) that *plays*, not actors, "ought to be 'the abstract and brief chronicles of the time,' " that, when current history furnishes a good dramatic situation, the playwright should take advantage of it. He therefore calls his play "The Spanish Armada" and lays it before Tilbury Fort. Then he constructs his action after other fixed rules (as set out in Chapter 2 above), and the comedy turns, of course, upon his misunderstanding and misapplication of the rules to which he is the slave. He rejects all the right ones and champions all the wrong ones. He rejects, for example, every received canon of exposition, imagining no pre-play situation, acknowledging no commitment to motivation or probability. At one extreme, he sees his characters as lifeless puppets, lacking all identity beyond the lines they speak; at the other, he sees them as dictating the very thoughts of the actors who portray them. He has no understanding at all of mimetic art. He understands nothing of the covenants of fiction, the tactics for suspending disbelief. He understands nothing of his responsibility as a playwright to his audience or to his actors. And consequently his audience derides him, and his actors destroy his play. Of course, he is not wholly at fault since he has derived his rules from the plays he sees and since each of his follies indicts a widespread dramaturgical offense. But "The Spanish Armada" is nonetheless Puff's own play. It could be no one else's.

According to the fixed rules governing Puff's art, there "must be a procession," a "little of the masque" to cap off the tragedy (240); and the seventh section is therefore his closing scene, which he sets as follows: "*Flourish of drums — trumpets — cannon, &c. &c. Scene changes to the sea — the fleets engage — the musick plays 'Britons strike home.' — Spanish fleet destroyed by fire-ships, &c. — English fleet advances — musick plays 'Rule Britannia.' — The procession of all the English rivers and their tributaries with their emblems, etc. begins with Handels water music, ends with a chorus, to the march in Judas Maccabaeus.*"

Contemporary audiences genuinely enjoyed this spectacle. Such splendid processions had indeed captured the English fancy during the 1770's and Sheridan stages the sketch as much for its spectacular as for its burlesque values. To be sure, he makes the point that Puff's tragedy is none the better for these theatrical appendages; but he then infuses his own play *(The Critic* itself) with the celebratory spirit of the masque. Thus, even while burlesquing specific dramatic offenses, he generates a patriotic fervor that delights in its own boisterous excesses and gives rise to the jovial patriotic traditions of John Bull and Britannia with helmet and shield. To achieve the dual emphases of the sketch, Sheridan opens the procession in burlesque, presenting the Thames River with both its banks on one side, one crowned with alders, the other with a fancy villa. After elaborate coaching from Puff, Thames exits between his banks, thus to conclude the clearly burlesque features of the pageant. And, when the drop opens to reveal the engagement at sea (as represented in "a very natural manner," according to one account),[17] the legitimate masque takes over. But Sheridan keeps Puff on the scene, a buffoon who "*directs and applauds every thing.*" In this rousing patriotic masque, Puff has clearly wrought better than he knows; but his persisting buffoonery reminds the audience of his earlier artistic atrocities.

II *The Whole Play*

While the seven sketches assert discrete identities, they are successfully joined into an effective dramatic unit. The initial setting at Dangle's house encourages a parade of characters, for everyone has adequate reason to be there. The several sketches are carefully linked, for the introduction of one is usually worked into the conclusion of another. And the main characters, the Dangles, Sneer, and Puff, provide an obvious structural continuity for the entire play. The major characterizations formed in the first act, of course, closely determine the tone and content of the last two, and it is possibly because the first act so handsomely serves this generative function (as well as for its theatrical and topical variety) that Sheridan valued it above all else he wrote.[18] Less subtly, he secured unity among the several acts by having Puff's new tragedy mentioned prominently at the outset of the play in a newspaper account anticipating both the discourse on puffing in Act I and the rehearsal episodes in Acts II and III. Recurring political topics also enforce the unity of the play, as does the repeated insistence that actors and plays are the abstract and brief chronicles of the time.

Through the interplay of three literary modes — the comic, the satiric, and the burlesque (as noted above) — Sheridan deepens the dimensions of his total statement. In formal concept, for example, "The Spanish Armada" is simple burlesque; it parodies the conventions of a revered art form. But Sheridan stages it not merely for its burlesque values, however rich they may be, but also for its values to Puff's character. Seen as a product of Puff's mind, it dramatizes all the social and artistic follies his character displays. Consequently, Sheridan not only illustrates through it the atrocities of bad tragedy, as mere burlesque would do, but also reveals the crippled poetic behind these atrocities and indeed the impoverished understanding behind the poetic. As burlesque, then, Puff's little play stands upon a very broad base of satire.

Similarly, satire and comedy complement each other in Sheridan's management of character and situation. If comedy assumes a basically sympathetic posture, placing laughter and delight above corrective intent (though certainly not excluding it), then comedy dominates key moments in the play: Mrs. Dangle's dilemma with the foreign entertainers, Sheridan's joke on himself as a writing manager, Sneer's pointed innuendos during the rehearsal, and the joyous masque at the close. In other key moments, however, the corrective intent of satire strongly asserts itself. Although Dangle earns sympathy at last, the play certainly satirizes his indifferent patriotism, just as it satirizes Sir Fretful's pernicious vanity and the contemporary taste for foreign entertainment. The interplay of comedy and satire has the effect of abstracting and generalizing the corrective force of the play. Since, for example, the play mixes pointed satire and amiable comedy, it generates indignation less against Dangle personally than against dangling generally and against the conditions giving rise to dangling. By mixing comedy and satire, Sheridan deepens the implications of his theme; and such mixtures of mode obviously add richness and complexity to a basically linear and simple dramatic structure.

III   The Critic *as Criticism*

As criticism, *The Critic* attacks failings among audiences, critics, and playwrights; but it also points out correspondences between bad art and bad humanity. In criticizing audiences, it indicts the popular taste for sentimental drama and for foreign entertainments — taste that allows bad playwrights to flourish. In criticizing critics, it indicts excessive permissiveness on the one hand (through Dangle) and excessive censoriousness on the other (through Sneer). It also exposes the vanity prompting critics to arbitrate taste for the public, and it condemns the hypocrisy they practice in supporting their pretensions. The discourse on puffing in Act I elaborately damns irresponsible newspaper criticism of the sort that deliberately misleads the public, preying upon its mental and moral weaknesses.

And actually Mr. Puff's tragedy, the work of a critic-turned-playwright, criticizes critics in suggesting that they often misunderstand the art they criticize. Criticism of playwrights in *The*

Critic attacks personal vanity, which promotes testiness and hostility to all criticism, however sound; and, of course, it attacks incompetence of the sort illustrated by Puff's play. Each of Puff's "rules," as indicated above in Chapter 2, emphasizes a presiding flaw in contemporary tragedy. And the text of his play illustrates yet other flaws: improbable motivation, erratic characterization, fragmented dialogue, contrived argument, shallow pathos, inexact entrance and exit cues, eddying action, flabby verse.

The recurring patriotic appeals made by *The Critic* clearly indicate that the play does not limit its interests to theatrical matters. At the very outset, Mr. Puff's preoccupation with bad art corresponds to his flawed partiotism and in turn to his ineffective humanity. And Puff's chicanery infects the world of politics and commerce as well as the world of art. Through Puff, as a matter of fact, Sheridan makes his most penetrating observations upon art and life. As a professional puffer, Puff reduces deception to rule. Through intricate falsehoods, he offers to exploit human vanity; and he succeeds. As a playwright, he attempts similar stratagems: he reduces art to rule, applying to it the same dishonest principles he applies to life; and he fails. The point is, of course, that art resists deceit more successfully than life does; that, while art may flourish for a time in the hands of practical deceivers, it will eventually betray the deceivers in their deceit. First and last, art is an instrument of truth. It draws upon many forms and conventions — some of them spectacular and artificial, others scrupulously realistic — but always it supports and reveals truth.

As though to ratify these affirmations about art and truth, Sheridan seizes control of Puff's play at the close. He implies that masques have little legitimate place as appendages to tragedy; but he demonstrates that they serve important artistic ends when they function in their own right and celebrate honest human experiences. Throughout the play, Sheridan has emphasized the correlation between bad art and bad humanity, especially as expressed through flawed patriotism. At the close, in a splendid patriotic masque, he celebrates art's proper function as an instrument of honor and truth.

CHAPTER 8

Theatrical Miscellanea

A FTER entering Parliament in 1780, Sheridan gave little concentrated industry to his literary and theatrical careers. But, while his reputation as a dramatist rests chiefly upon four plays written between his twenty-third and twenty-eighth years, a few others — one antedating *The Rivals;* others dating from 1775 to 1808 — round out the record. Actually only three of these, *St. Patrick's Day* (1775), *A Trip to Scarborough* (1777), and *Pizarro* (1799), claim really serious literary or historical interest. The others represent Sheridan's sporadic managerial advising: his collaborations (usually to an undetermined extent) in afterpieces submitted to the theater; an occasional scenario sketched by him to be developed by someone else; at least one pantomine, *Robinson Crusoe* (1781), possibly attributable to his invention. And through the whole uneven record of his dramatic career runs the widely advertised promise of two full-length plays — one, a comedy; the other, a comic opera — neither of which he ever finished.

I *Two Unfinished Plays*

Off and on for almost twenty years, from 1778 to 1795, the London periodical press reported Sheridan at work on a comedy called *Affectation*.[1] Because passages of the surviving text use a camp jargon popular during the military encampment at Coxheath, 1778 - 79, Crompton Rhodes conjectures that Sheridan began work on the play immediately after staging *The School for Scandal*, possibly putting it aside to take up *The Camp* (an afterpiece on which he collaborated) and *The Critic*.[2] Extracts printed by Moore and Rhodes indicate that Sheridan intended his comedy to satirize many species of affectation, including affectations of business, accomplishments, love of letters, wit, intrigue, sensibility, vivacity, silence, importance, profligacy, and moroseness.[3] He had jotted these topics inside the cover of a memorandum book, adding on the first leaf the title, "Affectation," and following with the names of three characters, Sir Babble Bore, Sir Peregrine Paradox, and Feignwit. The remaining pages, a collection of character sketches and random fragments of wit, give no hint of the intended shape of the play or its action; but they do open engaging insights into Sheridan's imagination. They show his mind running as usual to comic contrasts and to striking, graphic humor. They also show the very language of his scenario just ready to burst forth into witty dialogue. One brief passage, describing a fat wife with her lean husband, will illustrate: "see them together, one's mast, and the other all hulk — she's a dome and he's built like a glass-house — when they part, you wonder to see the steeple separate from the church, and were they to embrace, he must hang round her neck like a skein of thread on a lace-maker's bolster."[4]

As much talked about as *Affectation*, and as eagerly awaited after 1778, is a comic opera called *The Foresters*. Rhodes surmises that this piece grew out of an unfinished sketch based upon Sir John Suckling's *The Goblins* and variously titled in Sheridan's version "A Wild Drama" and "A Drama of Devils."[5] If *The Foresters* is indeed a development from "A Drama of Devils," Sheridan's first work on it might have begun as early as 1770 when an edition of Suckling's plays appeared. Very possibly, says Rhodes, Sheridan abandoned his plan to adapt the Suckling play after discovering in it a germ for *Affectation*. In proceeding with the opera, then, he dropped the names and disguises of goblins from his scheme and made his characters simply freebooters who live in a forest and prey upon the inhabitants of a nearby village (as the goblins of the original design had harried the villagers living near their forest).[6]

The new names chosen for the opera, such names as Oscar and Malvina, Morven and Colona, suggest the influence of James Macpherson's Ossian, as does some of the swollen language of the dialogue. But the Ossianic influence seems to go no farther; and surviving fragments fail to suggest a plot for the play. One fragment introduces the brothers Nico and Lubin, who both love the same proud maiden, Malvina, and both suffer her scorn. In a turn of typical Sheridanesque irony, the brothers grow so fond of their own romantic distresses that they actually welcome Malvina's rebuffs, hoping she will persevere in them. The "comic dolorousness" of this episode, as Rhodes calls it, suggests something of the spirit of the play, if little of its major line of action.[7]

Sheridan's classic indolence, complicated by his Parliamentary duties, probably accounts for his failure to finish the two long-awaited plays. But Michael Kelly, musician for Drury Lane, advances in his *Reminiscences* another theory of the matter. In his view, Sheridan failed to complete the two pieces because he came at last to fear the author of *The School for Scandal*, to fear, that is, that he might taint his reputation by failing to compete successfully with himself.[8]

II *Some Collaborations*

Well before he needed to face that fear, however, he entered into the first of his theatrical collaborations, perhaps the most important one apart from *The Duenna*, the composition of the burlesque burletta *Ixion*. In August, 1770, his school friend Nathaniel Brassey Halhed had sent him a manuscript copy of the piece. It was then called "Jupiter," and like Kane O'Hara's *Midas* (1764), after which it was patterned, it presented "musical parodies upon a heathen fable,"[9] featuring one lively intrigue between Jupiter and Mrs. Amphitryon (the wife of Major Amphitryon) and another between Sir Richard Ixion and Juno, who finally substitutes Miss Peggy Nubilis for herself in the affair. In response to Halhed's request that he revise the piece, Sheridan changed the title to *Ixion*, following the reductive spirit of burlesque, and cast the whole play in the frame of a rehearsal. He let Halhed's original situations supply the rehearsal episodes; then he added a trio of commentators much like those he would later draw for *The Critic*. Thus Simile in *Ixion* seems a "dim and shadowy pre-existence" (in Moore's phrase)[10] of Puff, just as O'Cullin and Monopoly foreshadow Dangle and Sir Fretful Plagiary. Sichel writes that the piece was submitted unsuccessfully both to Samuel Foote, for the Haymarket, and to Garrick, for Drury Lane.[11] But on the testimony of a letter expressing fears that the failure of a comparable piece, Thomas Bridge's *Dido*, might foredoom the success of *Ixion*, Moore reckons that the young authors declined to offer their play for production anywhere.[12] In any case, it was never staged.

Sichel senses Sheridan's hand in a wide variety of later collaborations — Tickell's *The Carnival of Venice* (1781); James Cobb's pantomime *Harlequin Hurly Burly* (1785); Burgoyne's *The Heiress* (1786); Sédaine's *Richard Coeur de Lion* (translated by Burgoyne in 1786); Dittersdorf's *The Doctor and the Apothecary* (translated by James Cobb in 1788). Cecil Price discusses quite a few other pieces, plays showing revisions in Sheridan's handwriting and his notes of managerial advice. During his Drury Lane years, however, his offices as collaborator involved him chiefly in four works: a "musical entertainment" called *The Camp;* an operatic romance called *The Forty Thieves;* a German melodrama, *The Stranger;* and a musical afterpiece *The Glorious First of June.*[13] *The Camp* sets its intrigues in and around the military installation established at Coxheath late in 1778. Presented in two acts, it sharply satirizes the dishonest sutlers and contractors who shamelessly cheat the soldiers at the camp. It also satirizes, though good naturedly, the current vogues for camp jargon and camp dress; and it derides French cowardice while championing the patriotism of the selfless English recruits. Much of the comedy turns on the dilemmas of a painter of theatrical scenery, an Irishman named O'Daub, who gets himself arrested as a spy while trying to locate a perspective from which to sketch the camp for a backdrop at Drury Lane. And a sentimental reunion motif, involving a stalwart English yeoman and his girl back home, adds sweetening to the piece.

From its opening on October 15, 1778, until the publication of Tate Wilkinson's *The Wandering Patentee* in 1795, *The Camp* was universally attributed to Sheridan. Quite arbitrarily, however, Wilkinson denied Sheridan's authorship, declaring the piece a performance unworthy of his talent. And Moore, on discovering a copy in Richard Tickell's handwriting, assigned it to Tickell. Sichel accepts Moore's attribution and, like Moore, assumes that Sheridan might have retouched the piece a bit for Tickell; but Allardyce Nicoll and Crompton Rhodes yet see *The Camp* as chiefly Sheridan's, possibly written in collaboration with General John Burgoyne, whose *The Maid of the Oaks; or, The Fête Champêtre* had earlier featured the painter O'Daub.[14]

External evidence denying Sheridan major authorship of *The Camp* is certainly inconclusive; and the internal qualities of the piece, while certainly not approaching Sheridan's best work, clearly reflect his touch. Jean Dulck aptly notes the kinship in manner and language between Lady Sneerwell and the three *grandames* of *The Camp*, Lady Plume, Miss Gorget, and Lady Sash.[15] Their effete companion, Sir Harry Bouquet, speaks pure Sheridanese in saying of the camp (and ironically too), "here's all the pride, pomp, and circumstance of glorious war! Mars in a *vis-à-vis*, and Bellona giving a Fête Champêtre" (p. 297). After the manner of *The Duenna*, the songs in *The Camp* neatly complement and extend the dialogue; but most Sheridanesque of all is the representation of villainy in the piece. The French turncoat Boulard, who has "too much honour to leave de English while dey do vin de battle," is cousin in self-acknowledged treachery to Snake, as is the shameless "con-man" Gage, who sells quicklime to the troops for hair powder and causes their hair to burn off during a rainstorm.

Except for the one character borrowed from Burgoyne, *The Camp* may well be Sheridan's own. But his shares in *The Glorious First of June*, *The Stranger*, and *The Forty Thieves* are by no chance so ample. For *The Glorious First of June*, as a matter of fact, he sketched only a rough scenario, which he then handed to James Cobb for dialogue. Yet other people, including the Duke of Leeds, Lord Mulgrave, and Joseph Richardson, supplied songs for the piece.[16] It was thrown together in two weeks and produced on July 2, 1794, to celebrate one of Lord Howe's naval victories. As extracted by Moore, Sheridan's scenario centers upon poor Susan, who pines for young Henry, her true love then at sea with Howe. The scenes reveal (1) Susan at the fair, (2) Susan on a solitary walk, (3) Susan meeting a gypsy fortune teller, and (4) Susan's ultimate reunion with Henry, which takes place after a sea battle magnificently staged by De Loutherbourg and splendidly accompanied by a choral rendition of "Rule Britannia."[17] To celebrate another naval victory, the one at Cape St. Vincent in 1797, this piece was renamed *Cape St. Vincent* and revived three years later at Drury Lane, just months before the appearance of *The Stranger*.

Moore's friend Mr. Rogers had heard Sheridan claim "on two different occasions" to have written *The Stranger* "from beginning to end."[18] But this statement is a bold exaggeration, probably meant to suggest the headaches encountered in shaping for production the work of a rank amateur. Benjamin Thompson, an unsuccessful lawyer, had submitted the play to Sheridan in 1798, a literal translation of Kotzebue's *Menschenhass und Reue* (1789). And Sheridan's share in it, acknowledged as "alterations and additions" in Thompson's advertisement, reflects a managerial concern for what will work theatrically. In a brief historical account of "*Menschenhass und Reue* in English," Myron Matlaw characterizes Sheridan's changes as follows: (1) he abridged or omitted repetitious, superfluous, and excessively sentimental scenes and speeches, together with those detrimental to plot development; (2) he added two "musical and pastoral" interludes: a dance at the end of Act II, and a brief scene at the beginning of Act IV; (3) for these interludes he added a dancing group and two singers, one called Anette, the other Savoyard; (4) he made minor improvements in plot, largely to suppress ill-placed and vulgar comedy and to refine upon tone.[19] About a year and a half before Thompson's version appeared, another translator, Schink, had submitted his rendering to Sheridan, only to have it returned eight days later with a notation that the management "did not think it would succeed in representation." When the play indeed appeared, Schink immediately charged plagiarism; but, in view of the liberties he had taken with the main conflict, the charge held little merit. *Menschenhass und Reue* is about an adulterous wife's ultimate reconciliation with her merciful and loving husband. In deference to English sensibilities, Schink had substituted the mere intention of adultery for the act itself. Thus he had robbed the play of the controversial theme which was to promote its great success in England, a success which for a time turned the English stage "stark German" and led to Sheridan's own adaptation of Kotzebue's *Die Spanier in Peru* just one year later.[20]

For *The Forty Thieves*, as for *The Glorious First of June*, Sheridan seems to have supplied only a rough scenario, which his collaborators then followed rather casually. The play, a two-act "operatical romance," adapts the Ali Baba story from *The Thousand and One Nights;* and added for spectacle are the elaborate rituals of Ardinelle and Orcobrand, the forces for Good and Evil who influence the actions of the mortals. According to Rhodes, this added apparatus provides an important pattern for the abstract moral conflicts embellishing the Christmas "speaking pantomimes" of the Victorian theater. Rhodes also sees *The Forty Thieves*, with its forest setting and its band of cutthroats, as the final glimmering of Sheridan's great plan for *The Foresters*.[21] John Genest notes that Sheridan's brother-in-law, Ward, first supplied dialogue for the scenario but managed it so badly that the younger Colman had to redo it.[22] Moore credits Ward with the dialogue and Colman with "an infusion of jokes."[23] But, whatever the distribution of tasks, the opera was staged with eminent success in April, 1806. After 1806, Sheridan seems to have involved himself (very slightly) in only one other collaborative effort, a three-act drama called *The Siege of St. Quintin*, which appeared at Drury Lane on November 10, 1808.

III *An Interlude and a Pantomime*

Very much in the facile spirit of his lesser collaborations, Sheridan sketched scenarios for two dumb shows, an interlude (1780) for

Henry Woodward's popular pantomime *Harlequin Fortunatus; or, the Wishing Cap*, and a full-length pantomime (1781) based loosely on Defoe's *Robinson Crusoe*. The earlier piece, called "The Storming and Taking of Fort Omoa," centers upon the singular gallantry of a British sailor who at the battle of Porto Omoa in October, 1779, graciously spared the life of an enemy soldier, whom he had first provided with a cutlass and then overcome in fair combat.[24] An account of the interlude printed in *The London Chronicle* for 1 - 4 January, 1780, describes De Loutherbourg's representation of "the inside of the Fort, with the guns mounted, the exterior of one of the bastions, with the fosse and counterscarp, and the harbour and British fleet." The scenes show (1) the British sailors scaling the outworks of the fort and securing them; (2) the special gallantry of the magnanimous young sailor, re-enacted inside the fort; and (3) the surrender of the fort by the Governor of San Fernando de Omoa. Mr. Vernon's rendition of "Rule Britannia," with choral accompaniment, concludes the piece.[25]

The Lady's Magazine for the following January (1781) carries "an Account of the new Pantomime called *Robinson Crusoe; or, Harlequin Friday* performed at Drury Lane Theatre on January 20th."[26] This account reveals that, in writing his one full-length pantomime, Sheridan departed markedly from his supposed source. Only the first of the three parts borrows significantly from Defoe. It presents the landing of savages with Friday on Crusoe's island; Crusoe's putting them to rout and saving Friday's life; and the arrival of a mutinous English crew whose captain, when restored to command by Crusoe, ultimately takes everyone on the island to Cadiz. After arrival in Cadiz, Friday becomes Harlequin; and the second and third parts of the pantomime dramatize his efforts to marry Columbine, the daughter of a merchant, Pantaloon, who had been shipwrecked on Crusoe's island. In the process, Harlequin tries to spirit Columbine into a nunnery, is discovered disguised as a friar, is tried before the Inquisition, condemned to die at the stake, and saved only by the miraculous intervention of his guardian witch, by whose influence Cadiz becomes a kind of elysium and Pantaloon blesses the marriage of Harlequin and Columbine.

Horace Walpole faulted the piece for incoherence, finding it sadly "unlike the pantomimes of Rich, which are full of wit! and coherent, and carried in a story!"[27] And the *European Magazine* for February, 1782, found it, "inferior to the worst performance of Mr. Messink,"[28] the pantomimist for Covent Garden. But the appearances of three London editions of the scenario, in 1781, 1789, and 1797, attests to the popularity of the piece throughout the remainder of the century.[29]

IV A Farce: St. Patrick's Day

In at least one instance, with the production of *St. Patrick's Day; or, the Scheming Lieutenant* on May 2, 1775, Sheridan distinguished himself as a writer of afterpieces. As a special compliment to the comedian Larry Clinch, whose performance as Sir Lucius had saved *The Rivals* on January 28, he prepared in this farce an acting *tour de force* in which the male lead plays three roles: an Irish lieutenant, an oafish peasant, and a German quack. Disguised in turn as peasant and quack, the lieutenant manages to secure for himself the daughter of a crusty jurist, Justice Credulous, who violently mistrusts military men and goes to any length to protect his daughter from them. It was a perfect vehicle for Clinch's benefit performance that spring and was well enough received to justify five additional performances before summer.[30]

Certainly Sheridan loaded *St. Patrick's Day* with the weariest conventions of farce: the double disguise, the tyrannical father, the shrewish wife, the incorrigible daughter. He bothers little with motivation, allows sudden and illogical resolutions of conflict, sacrifices character to caricature, and subordinates everything to extravagant situation. *The London Magazine* for May, 1775, properly enough complains that "His canvass is certainly filled with the likeness of no human creature in existence."[31] But *St. Patrick's Day* opens some important insights into Sheridan's sense of the comic. Here emerge more noticeably than in the longer plays some arresting strains of dark humor, cruel thrusts at man's predatory follies, jokes ridiculing mortality and suffering, and touches of sexual innuendo. The laughter provoked by the play is hearty enough, but it is not carefree laughter: its implications tap reservoirs of pain and outrage.

The heroine, Lauretta, for example, rhapsodizes about the "bold upright youth, who makes love to-day, and has his head shot off to-morrow" (151). She loves the "sweet fellows" who "sleep on the ground, and fight in silk stockings and lace ruffles" (151). But her mother, Mrs. Bridget, warns her against marrying a soldier, who might return from battle "like a Colossus, with one leg at New York and the other at Chelsea Hospital" (151). Justice Credulous is reported to prefer seeing "his daughter in a scarlet fever, than in the arms of a soldier" (147). His wife would prefer following him to the grave to seeing him owe his life "to any but a regular-bred physican" (167). Lieutenant O'Connor, reflecting on some ragged recruits, dourly laments the irony that "these poor fellows should scarcely have bread from the soil they would die to defend" (147). And one of the wretched yeomen, faced with recruitment, stumbles through the melancholy line "my relations be all dead, thank heavens, more or less" (156).

It is macabre comedy, comedy toughened by reference to eager wantonness (150), even to phallic erection (165). And it is darkened still more by the lugubrious babbling of Dr. Rosy, the lieutenant's friend, who rings constant changes on the theme of mortality, remembering bygone happy years with his wife Dolly, whose rotting and aching teeth he once so delighted to pull. Through the whole play, he intones his *memento mori:* "flesh is grass . . . flowers fade . . . Life's a shadow . . . Thick-sighted mortals . . . Wandering in error . . . Futurity is dark . . . Men are Moles."

If not through characterization or motivation, then, Sheridan certainly complicates through dark humor the total comic quality of *St. Patrick's Day.* The piece presupposes man's ability to delight in his own wicked enormities, to laugh at his wars, his lusts, his class injustices, his wantonness and selfishness — even to laugh at physical decay and impending death — an unsavory laughter evoked by (and from) unsavory people. Tradition has it that Sheridan wrote *St. Patrick's Day* in forty-eight hours, striking it off in a white creative heat. If indeed it represents a relatively spontaneous creativity, it shows the young playwright indulging a Jonsonian satiric fancy, a judgmental comic vision rarely indulged in in his major comedies.

V   *An Adaptation from Vanbrugh:* A Trip to Scarborough

If *St. Patrick's Day* allows dark humor and indulges in sexual innuendo, certainly *A Trip to Scarborough* does neither. Its intent, as a matter of fact, is to cleanse Sir John Vanbrugh's dirty Restoration comedy *The Relapse* (1696) and thus make it palatable to an audience in 1777. Soon after taking over management of Drury Lane, Sheridan had adapted three of Congreve's comedies, *The Old Bachelor* (performed on November 19, 1776), *Love for Love* (November 29), and *The Way of the World* (December 31). But apparently no record of his revisions survives; and contemporary periodical accounts, which show disappointment in the productions, complain of general miscasting and inexpert use of the Drury Lane company. The adaptation from Vanbrugh, however, appeared fairly successfully on February 24, 1777, and managed a run of nine performances, despite an inauspicious first two nights.[32]

Rhodes observes rather ingeniously that Sheridan's changes in Vanbrugh's *The Relapse* seem designed to correct the strictures made against it in Jeremy Collier's *Short View of the Immorality and Profaneness of the English Stage* (1698).[33] Collier attacks Vanbrugh's play on five fronts — misleading title, moral viciousness, ill-contrived plot, indecorous manners, and violation of the dramatic unities — [34] and it is true that Sheridan's revisions generally correct these kinds of failings, as might any such bowdlerization of Restoration comedy designed for the "delicate audiences" of the late 1770's.

The title of Vanbrugh's play denotes the relapse from marital fidelity of the disgraceful spark Loveless, who at the end of Colley Cibber's *Love's Last Shift*, to which *The Relapse* is a sequel, had sworn new constancy to his faithful wife Amanda, whom he had abandoned ten years before. In *The Relapse*, Loveless effects a liaison with Berinthia, Amanda's best friend; and Amanda, suspecting her husband's renewed infidelity but not knowing with whom, considers having an affair with Berinthia's former lover, Mr. Worthy, whom she at last refuses. A second plot, and one of equal importance, finds an impoverished younger brother, Young Fashion, scheming to marry the wealthy but enormously countrified Miss Hoyden, daughter of the boorish squire, Sir Tunbelly Clumsey. In securing Hoyden for himself, Young Fashion must pose as his own older brother, the fatuous and shamelessly uncharitable fop, Lord Foppington, to whom the girl is originally promised. And the complications of this stratagem are resolved only after poor Hoyden has actually married both brothers. Matters at last fall out profitably for Young Fashion, who proves (with the help of Bull the chaplain) that his own marriage to Hoyden had taken place before his brother's.

In grumbling about the title of Vanbrugh's play, Collier argues sarcastically that *The Younger Brother; or, The Fortunate Cheat* would better have served. Sheridan offers yet a better alternative by choosing a title proper to the setting of the play, rather than favoring either of the plots. His title also represents revisions in the direction of unity; for, while Vanbrugh's action starts at the house of Loveless in the country, moves first to London, thence to Sir Tunbelly's house, and so back to London, Sheridan's takes place wholly in Scarborough, a resort town to which his people have come for proper enough reasons: Loveless and Amanda for a second honeymoon,

Berinthia to meet Townly (Vanbrugh's Worthy), Foppington to marry Hoyden, and Young Fashion to confront his brother.

And in the interest of unity Sheridan makes other fine changes. In the first place, he tightens continuity by cutting out unnecessary scenes. Thus he omits Vanbrugh's Act I, scene 1, at Loveless' country retreat, and he opens his own play at the second scene of the original, the scene introducing Young Fashion and his man Lory. By having Young Fashion come upon Townly in this scene, Sheridan supplies exposition explaining the Townly-Amanda intrigue, the Foppington-Amanda interest (which ultimately results in sword play between Foppington and Loveless), and the imminent marriage of Foppington to Miss Hoyden — all this information implied or reported by Townly. And, by having Townly suggest here that Young Fashion get Hoyden for himself, Sheridan triggers one of the mainsprings of action in the play. Similar effects of economy and continuity result from the excision of Vanbrugh's Act III, scene 5, in which Young Fashion seeks permission to marry Hoyden without delay. Sheridan proceeds directly to Act IV, scene 1, and motivates the urgent marriage by having Lory bring news of Foppington's early arrival at Sir Tunbelly's house.

In a second unifying strategy, and one which complements the first, Sheridan rearranges or completely reconceives key episodes of the original play. Consequently, Vanbrugh's Act IV, scene 6, in which Foppington is dragged in, accused of imposture, bound and thrown among the dogs, becomes Sheridan's climax to Act V, though Sheridan saves his Foppington from the kennels. And with telling modifications, Vanbrugh's Act V, scene 4, in which Amanda finally rejects Worthy, becomes Sheridan's Act V, scene 1, in which Amanda rejects Townly while Berinthia and Loveless watch from the shrubbery. All other action in Vanbrugh's fifth act — Berinthia's stratagem as procurer for Worthy and Young Fashion's successful bribery of Bull the chaplain — falls victim to Sheridan's ax, in being quite outside his design. And, since Foppington's disgrace dominates Sheridan's closing scene, Sheridan neatly executes his finale by having the entire Loveless party arrive for nuptial festivities at Sir Tunbelly's house, to which Foppington had earlier invited them, rather than at Foppington's own lodging back in London, as Vanbrugh manages it in his Act V. This expedient also coolly eliminates the role of Sir John Friendly, who enters Vanbrugh's play only to identify Lord Foppington at the end of Act IV, an office readily enough served by the Loveless party in Act V of Sheridan's play.

Sheridan's version is nine large scenes shorter than Vanbrugh's; and it is more efficient than his, more shapely; structurally, it is much tighter; and it is squeaky clean. Collier's strictures against *The Relapse* can nowhere touch its scrupulous high morality; for, in cleaning the play, Sheridan removes every hint of sexual innuendo, coarse frankness, or playful irreverence. First of all, he converts Old Coupler, the homosexual pander, into a distant kinswoman of Sir Tunbelly and a friend of Young Fashion. He completely omits Vanbrugh's outrageous Chaplain Bull, who permits Hoyden's double marriage; and with Bull goes all the satire against spurious apologetics and clerical profligacy. The only talk of double marriage in Sheridan's play comes of the possibility that Hoyden must marry Young Fashion twice, once secretly and once publicly. And the original Hoyden's eager anticipation of double wedding nights (IV, 1) is, of course, disallowed. While Vanbrugh's Foppington delights to recall his own father's death, Sheridan's more decorously recalls the death of an uncle. And, while Vanbrugh's Nurse "rips up" the story of how the infant Hoyden once used to "hang on this poor tett, and suck and squeeze, and kick and sprawl . . . till the belly on't was so full it would drop off like a leech" (IV, 1), Sheridan's only boasts of giving Hoyden "pure good milk" (IV, 1). Sheridan declines even to allow his Hoyden to contrast her own confinement at Sir Tunbelly's house to the liberty of the greyhound bitch running free about the yard. And, while Vanbrugh's Young Fashion sees Fortune as a bitch, Sheridan's scrupulously ennobles her to a jilt.

But certainly Sheridan's most telling bowdlerization occurs in his alteration of Vanbrugh's Act IV, scene 3, in which Loveless consummates his affair with Berinthia by carrying her off to the couch in her closet while she calls out very softly "Help, help, I'm ravished, ruined, undone! O Lord, I shall never be able to bear it." When Sheridan's Loveless invites Berinthia into the closet, she not only refuses to accompany him but swears never to trust herself in a room with him while she lives. Instead, they make arrangments to meet later on the lawn — where again no liaison is cemented. Sheridan's assault on this scene cuts out the heart of Vanbrugh's play.

For reasons other than bowdlerization, Sheridan makes numerous lesser changes in Vanbrugh's play. Young Fashion's colloquy with the waterman in *The Relapse* about barge passage (I, 2) becomes in Sheridan's play (and for obvious reasons) a dispute with the post-boy over the post fare. In revising Lord Foppington's famous dressing room scene (Vanbrugh's I, 3), Sheridan brings foppish fashions up to date, emphasizing the cut of the coat rather than the length of the pockets, the jewelry rather than the periwig. And, at the close of the scene, he sends Foppington not to take his seat in Parliament but to dine at Donner's, a restaurant in Scarborough well known to Sheridan's audience. Possibly for theatrical-managerial reasons, he disallows Foppington's references (in II, 1) to drafty theater buildings and causes him to talk instead of going to the opera to enjoy his gossip circle, which Vanbrugh has him enjoying in church. And because Sheridan's scenic cuts excise some bright passages of wit, he occasionally salvages a good line and works it into another scene, perhaps even gives it to a different character, as he does in combining the two fragments of *The School for Scandal.*

Jean Dulck, who reads *A Trip to Scarborough* quite sympathetically, regards Sheridan as succeeding in his basic plan to convert frank Restoration bawdry into the warm, amiable comedy of the late century, the kind of comedy apparent in *The Rivals* and in *The Duenna.*[35] Sheridan has his Loveless call this transmutation "a little wholesome pruning" effected by one possessing the modesty to believe that "we should preserve all we can of our deceased authors" (II, 1). But it is really impossible to see that Sheridan succeeds by his own standards. Putting aside the lackluster language of *A Trip to Scarborough* — an emasculation of Vanbrugh's language — there are the problems of super-subtle and contrived motives in the action. In Sheridan's Act IV, scene 2, for example, Berinthia lectures Amanda in these terms: "while you suffer Townly to imagine that you do not detest him for his designs on you, you have no right to complain that your husband is engaged elsewhere." This speech and others like it represent Sheridan's effort to translate the hard sexual intrigue of *The Relapse* into a bland social byplay in which four moralists offer to make one another a bit jealous, but always on a plane of high morality. The worst offense comes, of course, in the scene on the lawn in Act V where the whole precious intrigue is canceled for sentimental reasons. Amanda declares her fidelity to Loveless; Townly, his to Berinthia. Berinthia and Loveless, who watch all this from the shadows, declare a mutual shame for a theoretical and inconsequential guilt; and honor triumphs all round.

Similarly arbitrary and unsatisfactory is the resolution of the second action, the final scene of the play, in which Young Fashion simply confesses his stratagems, Sir Tunbelly promises Hoyden a fortune (in a fit of pique against Foppington), and Foppington assumes a philosophic air and goes home. Actually, then, neither of the main actions resolves itself; both just dissolve in a tissue of reassessed motives. Sheridan casually sidesteps all the major issues of Vanbrugh's play: its close analysis of human sexuality, its tough satire against aristocratic preferment and clerical profligacy, and its indictment of the laws of primogeniture. All this content Sheridan sacrifices to high moral scruples on the one hand and low buffoonery on the other. He was right to upbraid himself years later for meddling with Restoration comedy.[36]

VI *An Adaptation from Kotzebue:* Pizarro

Mr. Dangle in *The Critic* fulminates against theatrical audiences for whose tender scruples Vanbrugh and Congreve "undergo a bungling reformation" (I, 1, p. 197). Mr. Puff in that same play rejoices in the bluster of his wild pseudo-tragedy: "Now then for my magnificence! — my battle! — my noise! — and my procession!" (III, 1, p. 239). In these two speeches Sheridan looks before and after — back to his earlier offenses against Vanbrugh; forward to his own blustering pseudo-tragedy, *Pizarro.* Even opening-night critics at Drury Lane, on May 24, 1799, perceived shocking similarities between *Pizarro* and Mr. Puff's "The Spanish Armada."[37] The fustian speeches, the sentimental heroines, the vaguely motivated situations, the exaggerated heroes, the magnificence, the battle, the noise, and the procession — all the flagrant tactlessness of Puff's play was here. But the people loved it. In pushing, crushing mobs they demanded thirty-one performances of it in what remained of the season. And it became a favorite repertory piece for a good half-century to come.[38]

The play succeeded for several clear reasons, all of them certainly anticipated by Sheridan. As a translation of Kotzebue's *Die Spanier in Peru,* first of all, it captured the current craze for German melodrama — the sudden and powerful appetite among theatergoers for broad, dark passion on the stage; for crosscurrents of jealousy and cruelty, bruised love and racking pathos. Sheridan himself had initiated this fad with the production of *The Stranger* in 1798, and he now gave the public more of the same with the production of *Pizarro.* He secured his success by writing for a brilliant cast: Mrs. Siddons as Elvira, Mrs. Jordan as Cora, John Philip Kemble as Rolla, Mr. Barrymore as Pizarro — full and flamboyant roles for the most popular and gifted members of the company. Finally, he amplified the appeal of the production by pointing up its political implications. *Die Spanier in Peru,* which dramatizes Pizarro's invasion of Peru in 1531, represents Pizarro as a fallen hero, a once-valiant warrior now turned tyrant. Driven by senseless ambition, he seeks to enslave a gentle and innocent people, to defile their temples, and to murder their king. The parallels with Napoleon's ambition and his threat to invade England immediately struck Sheridan's audiences; and in patriotic fervor they packed the theater, wildly applauding every hint of nationalistic sentiment in the piece.[39]

In adapting the play, Sheridan worked from a literal translation probably supplied him by a certain Maria Gassweiler.[40] He is said to have paid one hundred pounds to the translator, another hundred to a small-time blackmailer who threatened to produce his own version first, and yet another fifty to a bookseller in consideration for delaying the sale of Mrs. Anne Plumptre's translation. Since Sheridan possibly took a copy of the Plumptre translation with him from the bookseller's shop, he might have seen it before completing his own adaptation; but it is no longer thought to be his basic text.[41] His version, in any case, remains essentially faithful to Kotzebue's plot and theme; but it does evidence some telling theatrical changes, several minor refinements in plot, some subtle revision in characterization, and some quite major amplifications in language.

The theatrical changes chiefly add spectacle to the production. To accommodate spectacle, Sheridan simplified and abbreviated the scenic structure of Kotzebue's play, lopping off twenty scenic breaks, combining many short scenes into fewer longer ones, entirely omitting three substantial scenes in Act IV. He also reduced long speeches in an effort to buy time for magnificence, battle, noise, and procession.

Where Kotzebue calls in Act I for "The inside of Rolla's tent," Sheridan calls for a showy *"Pavilion near Pizarro's Tent";* where Kotzebue's Act III calls simply for a "free spot in a wood" (scenes 1 - 4), Sheridan's specifies *"A wild Retreat among stupendous Rocks."* And in Act V, scene 2, Sheridan calls not simply for "the outskirts of the camp" but for *"a Torrent . . . over which a Bridge is formed. A Fell'd Tree."* Completely original with Sheridan, and most spectacular of all, is the final scene of the play, Rolla's funeral in Act V, scene 4. It specifies *"A solemn March — Procession of Peruvian Soldiers, bearing Rolla's Body on a Bier, surrounded by Military Trophies. The Priests and Priestesses attending chaunt a Dirge over the Bier."* Such operatic moments also embellish the beginning of Act V when Cora sings a song written by Sheridan and set to Michael Kelly's music, a song of despair and love longing for her lost husband Alonzo. Similarly, Act III ends with a paean to the sun sung by

"*Priests and Priestesses at Sacrifice,*" and it opens with five Peruvian women singing a song "*expressive of their situation,*" a lamentation for their oppressed lot. Despite scenic cuts, then, new splendor, new music (mostly Michael Kelly's), and new scenery kept the first performance going for about five hours.[42]

In addition to operatic and scenic spectacle, Sheridan introduced powerful spectacular oratory, extravagant new speeches on political themes. The most striking such interpolation appears in Act II, scene 2, where the Peruvian warrior Rolla grandly contrasts Spanish godlessness to Peruvian virtue. Kotzebue allows here only a series of short speeches in which Rolla, Alonzo, and King Ataliba agree upon the proper motives of valor: love of country, king, and God (as demonstrated by the Peruvians but not by the Spaniards). Sheridan expands this lean colloquy into a fullblown harangue. Borrowing phrases and metaphors from his second speech against Warren Hastings, he causes Rolla to denounce the Spaniards (and by implication the French) for sacrilege, lust for power, arrogance, avarice, pride, tyranny, and lack of charity.[43] A procession of priests and virgins properly enough follows this harangue; then a fireball lights upon the altar while priests and virgins sing hymns to the sun. In Act V, scene 4, a similar oratorical addendum finds Elvira, Pizarro's mistress, warning the Spaniards that "the pursuit of avarice, conquest, and ambition never yet made a people happy or a nation great." Throughout the play, then, Sheridan pursues his design to turn Kotzebue's tragic German melodrama into a political-topical-oratorical-operatical, Anglo-Germanic tragedy.

That same design accounts for Sheridan's boldest change in the plot, the death of Pizarro in Act V, a detail true neither to Kotzebue nor to history, but one alike proper to poetic justice and to English expectations. In staging this episode, Sheridan causes some Spanish soldiers to find a path leading to the hiding place of the Peruvian women; and on this path Pizarro later meets his death. With other changes Sheridan supplied new exposition or enlivened action. Since, for example, Kotzebue's play is a sequel to his *Sonnenjungfrau*, he obviously assumed that his audience already knew about the love triangle involving Rolla, Cora, and Alonzo — in which Rolla finally gives up Cora to Alonzo. But Sheridan added this information through the role of an old cacique, Orozembo, who is captured by the Spaniards early in the play and brought before Pizarro. In Act II, Kotzebue places a boy in a tree to report the progress of battle; but Sheridan enlivens the action by having reports not only from the boy but also from embattled warriors who rush upon the scene. He also adds the detail of King Ataliba's capture and his rescue by Rolla.

One other change relates more closely to characterization than to plot. It excises the third, fourth, and fifth scenes of Kotzebue's Act IV, in which Elvira visits the imprisoned Alonzo and offers herself to him. Since Sheridan scrupulously ennobles Elvira's character, setting out to beatify a soldier's trull, he drops her first visit to the prison and uses only the second in which she urges Rolla, who has substituted himself for Alonzo, to murder Pizarro for the deliverance of mankind. Kotzebue's Elvira sells her virtue for the political influence she can command as Pizarro's mistress, but Sheridan's reverently bestows herself on Pizarro, the nation's idol, in a kind of patriotic gesture. As his tyranny grows, her curious patriotism gives place to remorse and penitence; and, at the end, she properly enough attires herself in a nun's habit. She is thoroughly sentimentalized by a sentimentalizing tendency which even touches Pizarro, for whom thought and memory in Sheridan's version become remorseful torment and whose more disgusting boasts, such as his threat to decapitate Alonzo's infant son, are carefully removed. Already hopelessly sentimental, Cora and Rolla undergo little change in the Englishing; but Sheridan does not allow his Cora, when deprived of the child later saved by Rolla, to deny the existence of God.

Supporting the added spectacle, new actions, and sentimental characterization of Sheridan's play is a highblown language quite foreign to Kotzebue's style. Moore sees this amplified rhetoric as deriving for the most part from the translator, much of whose diction went untouched into the final play.[44] But, quite irrespective of its origins, Sheridan seems to have liked the incantatory ring of the prose, some phrases of which scan as verse; indeed, he is said to have sat in a box at the theater and mouthed the fine speeches as he heard them.[45] What he created in *Pizarro* is a kind of hybrid monster, a political treatise toned up to high oratory and darkened by heavy tragic pathos. But for once in his life he combined in a single endeavor his energies as theater manager, playwright, patriot, and Parliamentarian. The endeavor held little promise as art, but it gave Richard Sheridan an immense personal satisfaction.

VII *Conclusion*

Despite the diversity of Sheridan's career, a broad general ethic seems to unify his major work. This ethic sees benevolence as the basic inclination of man and as his principal duty; and it calls reason to the support of benevolence. But it also recognizes that a simple benevolistic ethic does not immediately gratify man's sense of social achievement; that to gratify this sense man compromises and subverts his simple ethic and so lapses into folly. Since the answer to human folly is benevolence and since Sheridan (in promoting this answer) speaks as a benevolent man, his attitude to folly is essentially sympathetic and indulgent, promoting a comic view of the human condition. But his comedy always insists that folly can be dangerous, that the most innocent social pretensions can contain the seeds of cruelty and of savage tyranny. Consequently, the benevolence coloring his comic indictment of social folly also promotes his fierce indignation against tyranny and oppression.

Thematically, then, his work is much of a piece. The benevolistic ethic informing *The School for Scandal* touches as well the feminist premise of *The Rivals*, where charitable good sense struggles to supplant absolutism, vanity, and caprice. The malice of the Scandal College, the avarice and vanity of Don Jerome in *The Duenna*, and even the idle prejudice of Justice Credulous in *St. Patrick's Day* relate in their degree to the vicious cunning of Warren Hastings (as Sheridan characterizes him) and the aggressive despotism of Pizarro. And the same ideal of benevolent justice against which Hastings and Pizarro offend defines the goal of harmony toward which Sheridan's comedies reach.

The essential oneness of Sheridan's ethical vision appears nowhere more clearly than in the great Westminster Hall speech of 1788, the second of the major speeches against Hastings. In answering a proposition advanced earlier in the impeachment by his colleague Edmund Burke, Sheridan admits that, in a strange way, vice is indeed compatible with prudence — at least insofar as "prudence" is understood to mean the process of conducting through craft and resourcefulness a specific design to its conclusion. Caesar, Cromwell, and Philip of Macedonia give evidence that single-minded villainy can reach fruition through prudential management. But complex villainies, says Sheridan, effect their own defeat by quite overrunning all the controls of a governing prudence.[46] Like Joseph Surface, whose uncontrollable "avarice of crimes" brings him to a bad end in *The School for Scandal*, Hastings fares very well in his villainy so long as he devotes all his energies to one crime. But, when he begins to multiply his crimes, as Joseph does, he immediately foredooms his stratagems. Such multiple crimes, Sheridan argues, so aggravate hostile passions in the villain that he falls victim to his own divided self. In the virtuous man, the beneficent passions function in splendid harmony; they complement and expand one another, each fighting to establish its own supremacy in the will.[47]

Sheridan does not himself draw the analogy between Hastings and Joseph, but the theory of complex villainy applies so perfectly to them both that the speech comments perforce upon the play, both pieces revealing the same moral parentage — as if Sheridan saw in Hastings a true-life extension of Joseph, the comic and tragic minted from the same ore. For Sheridan, however, the tragic could never take lasting control over human affairs. For, while Providence does not exile evil from the world, it at least checks the spread of evil by contriving the demise of complex villainies. Since all villainy implies a pride too aggresive to content itself with a single crime, most villainy contains, as God would have it, the seeds of its own defeat.[48] Heaven smiles at last, with Sheridan, on the troubled affairs of men.

No doubt because of this essential moral optimism, Sheridan makes his audiences laugh at circumstances usually unpleasant to consciousness. As a rule, people prefer not to think of themselves as liars; yet throughout his comic canon Sheridan jokes amiably about man the liar. "I never scruple to lie to serve my Master," says Fag in *The Rivals*, "yet it hurts one's conscience to be found out" (I, 1, p. 43). The joke is absolutely typical of Sheridan, and it is funny because it treats with disarming candor a subject usually secreted from the consciousness of civilized man. In his heart of hearts man knows that he is a liar, that the circumstances of civilization sometimes require him to be; but he guards the knowledge from himself with subtle care, and he can face it squarely only when assisted by comedy, only when a burst of laughter relieves for an instant his pent-up moral anxiety. He has anxieties, too, about his own mortality, and Sheridan keeps him laughing at death jokes, jokes such as that in which Sir Lucius O'Trigger talks reassuringly of "snug" burials in the abbey (*Rivals*, V, 3, p. 106), and Justice Credulous, in *St. Patrick's Day*, deplores death, which "leaves a numbness behind that lasts a plaguy long time" (II, 4, p. 168). Civilized man also experiences persistent anxieties about his passionate nature, the incorrigible emotions that overwhelm his efforts at composed and rational conduct. He chafes inwardly at the social conventions which mechanize his spirit and diminish his humanity. Yet Sheridan makes him laugh at all the troublesome conditions of his subjective life and forces him to confront in comedy what he otherwise dares not think of.

The human understanding implied in these comic confrontations accounts importantly for Sheridan's durability as a comic playwright. Certainly his benevolistic ethic participates in the shape and spirit of his plays and gives form and direction to his new departures in comedy. But if he sought to revise the dramatic representation of benevolence in the English theater, he made little headway in the attempt. Ernest Bernbaum clearly enough records the resurgence of sentimental drama in the English theater after 1780, the ultimate triumph of sentimentality over Sheridan's kind of benevolistic comedy,[49] and the success of subsequent major playwrights cannot really be credited to his influence.

But his own best plays have flourished through the years without eclipse. In a fine essay about the American stage history of *The Rivals*, for example, Professor Mark S. Auburn notes three hundred eighty-eight performances in New York "from the production by Clinton's Thespians on April 21, 1778 to the production by Joseph Jefferson's company on January 6, 1894." Hundreds more were staged in Philadelphia and in other major American cities during the nineteenth century — to say nothing of frontier productions — and a sampling of professional productions in the twentieth century reveals no fewer than fifteen major revivals of *The Rivals* in England and America.[50] *The School for Scandal* enjoys a comparable lively popularity.[51]

Obviously, the plays continue successful because they are great acting pieces. They are "comedies of character," in Professor Auburn's phrase, and they appeal to great character actors. But this appeal could not endure if Sheridan's characters, however farcical some might seem, were really devoid of human substance. Ultimately, their address to life assures their durability. The world to them is a "given," and they do their best to make it work for them, or even to show themselves its master. In trying to succeed within, or against, it, some of them affect learning, some flash bravura, some show defiance, some bark authority, some melt sentimentally. Entangled in the contradictions of their own systems, manners, and delusions, they usually fail badly; but in these failures the audience sees its own secret experiences of life, its own failed schemes and ambitions. Thus its own covert foolishness becomes bearable to consciousness through the antics of the fools upon the stage. Sheridan's stage fools almost always claim some sympathy from the audience, and in learning to forgive them the audience learns to forgive itself — not so as to deceive itself or to claim moral superiority, but to forgive for a time its own incorrigible vanities, the better to live forthrightly and well.

If Sheridan's view of man is basically valid: if civilized man seeks generally to be good but finds his benevolence flawed by selfish aims, by offenses which afflict him with remorse, by anxieties which depress his fragile spirit, then Sheridan's kind of comedy must endure. It speaks to a need felt deeply by most people, a need for self-acknowledgment, for self-forgiveness, for freedom from anxiety and vague fear, a sense that in the long run all is well.

Notes and References

Chapter One

1. *The Letters of Richard Brinsley Sheridan*, ed. Cecil Price (Oxford, 1966), III, 77 - 78.

2. James Boswell quoting Samuel Johnson, *The Life of Samuel Johnson, L. L. D.*, ed. G. B. Hill and L. F. Powell (Oxford, 1934 - 1950), III, 116.

3. Although creditors were at the door at the time of Sheridan's death, Mrs. Sheridan protested that the family was not indigent. The stocks given by Sheridan to his second wife as a marriage settlement had been made inaccessible to him until the interest had accumulated forty thousand pounds. Sheridan had refused to unbind himself from this settlement, even though his father-in-law had urged him to do so.

4. Walter Sichel, *Sheridan* (London, 1909), I, 221.

5. Biographers disagree as to the month of Sheridan's birth. Some say late September; others, October. No documents confirm either date. See Thomas Moore, *Memoirs of the Life of the Rt. Hon. Richard Brinsley Sheridan* (New York, 1853), I, 9; R. Crompton Rhodes, *Harlequin Sheridan* (Oxford, 1933), p. 8.

6. Quoted by Moore, I, 10.

7. Sichel, I, 245.

8. Dr. Parr to Thomas Moore, August 3, 1818. Quoted in Moore, I, 13.

9. Rhodes, *Harlequin*, p. 11. The phrase is quoted from Thomas Creevey's account of a conversation with Sheridan in 1805.

10. Rhodes, *Harlequin*, p. 18 (from the testimony of Sheridan's sister Alicia).

11. Rhodes, *Harlequin*, p. 21. Sheridan speaking to Thomas Creevey.

12. The tradition arises from an account by Sheridan's sister Alicia. See Sichel, I, 344.

13. As quoted in Moore, I, 53.

14. A scene of the piece is reprinted in Moore, I, 199 - 200. Extended discussion of the juvenile work left among Sheridan's papers appears in Sichel, Chapter III, I, 270 - 317. The present discussion draws upon transcriptions of the juvenilia in Sichel and Moore. Extracts from the letters of Sheridan's

friend Halhed appear in W. Fraser Rae, *Life of Richard Brinsley Sheridan* (New York, 1896), I, 95 - 101.

15. A third satiric treatise, formulated like the other two as a Letter-to-the-Editor, actually appeared in *The Public Advertiser* for October 16, 1769. All three pieces are printed in *Letters*, I, 3 - 18.

16. Sheridan to his father, August 30, 1772, *Letters*, I, 35.

17. See Sichel, I, 400 - 401.

18. For the letters to Grenville, see *Letters*, I, 43 - 83, *passim.*, covering a period from late September, 1772, to May 14, 1773, according to Price's dating.

19. Sichel, I, 412 - 13, describes the essays on Temple and Blackstone.

20. As quoted in Sichel, I, 413 - 14.

21. The best attempt to recount Sheridan's career at the Middle Temple appears in Jerome B. Landfield's unpublished doctoral dissertation, "The Speeches of Richard Brinsley Sheridan Against Warren Hastings" (University of Missouri, 1958), pp. 53 - 54. Sheridan was never called to the bar; but an R. B. Sheridan paid dining fees at Middle Temple from January 30, 1774, to June 29, 1776.

22. Sichel, I, 471.

23. As quoted in Sichel, I, 474. Extracts also appear in Moore, I, 101 - 104, and Rae, I, 308.

24. Moore, I, 88.

25. Sichel (I, 523) declares the sum to be 31,500 pounds.

26. Sheridan to Thomas Linley, December 31, 1775, *Letters*, I, 95.

27. Garrick to Thomas King, July 17, 1777, *Letters of David Garrick,* ed. David M. Little and George M. Kahrl (Cambridge, Mass., 1963), p. 1171; Kitty Clive to David Garrick, March 22, 1778, as quoted in Rhodes, *Harlequin*, p. 78.

28. Rhodes, *Harlequin*, pp. 100 - 101, quoting "Mr. King's Address to the Public."

29. See Percy Fitzgerald, *The Lives of the Sheridans* (London, 1886), II, 236 - 37.

30. As quoted in Rhodes, *Harlequin*, 174 - 75. In his "Summary of Other Letters" *(Letters*, III, 256 - 65), Price lists ninety-eight such items.

31. See Moore, II, 259 - 61.

32. Fitzgerald, II, 13.

33. Charles Beecher Hogan, ed. *The London Stage, 1660 - 1800, Part V* (Carbondale, Ill., 1968), I, clxvii - clxviii.

34. Ibid., I, clxviii.

35. Ibid., I, clxxi. Mr. Hogan's calendar for the seasons mentioned indicates the number of performances recorded for each play.

36. See the Drury Lane and Covent Garden accounts as summarized throughout *The London Stage* at the beginning of each seasonal calendar for which the records yet survive.

37. Rhodes, *Harlequin*, p. 228.

38. See Fitzgerald, I, 192; Moore, II, 285.
39. Sheridan to Whitbread, November 1, 1812, *Letters*, III, 163. See also Quentin Skinner,. "Sheridan and Whitbread," *Theatre Notebook*, XVII (1963), 74 - 79.
40. See Sichel, I, 593 for some discussion of Sheridan's contributions. Also see footnotes to *Letters*, III, 308.
41. This summary of Sheridan's political creed derives directly from Michael T. H. Sadler, *The Political Career of Richard Brinsley Sheridan* (Oxford, 1912), pp. 28 - 29.
42. Moore (I, 184 - 89) dates the pamphlet on "Absentee Landlords" (apparently never published) as 1778 and quotes generous portions of it. Together with *The Critic*, the pamphlet on Indian affairs was one of "two things" of his Sheridan actually approved for printing. See Sheridan to His Wife [15 Oct. 1814?], *Letters*, III, 202.
43. Lucyle Werkmeister. *The London Daily Press, 1772 - 1792* (Lincoln, Nebraska, 1963), pp. 13 - 14; 71, and throughout.
44. See Jerome B. Landfield. "Sheridan's Maiden Speech: Indictment by Anecdote," *Quarterly Journal of Speech*, XLIII (1957), 141 - 42.
45. Moore, I, 228.
46. This assessment of Sheridan's habits as a speaker draws heavily upon Robert T. Oliver, *Four Who Spoke Out: Burke, Fox, Sheridan, Pitt* (Syracuse, N. Y., 1946), pp. 104 - 106; 144 - 47.
47. Contemporary comment quoted by Lewis Gibbs, "Sheridan Against Warren Hastings, *Quarterly Journal of Speech* XXXIV (1948), 467.
48. As quoted by Sadler, p. 44.
49. R. B. Sheridan, "Warren Hastings on the Begum Charge," in *Select British Eloquence*, ed. Chauncey H. Goodrich (New York, 1963), p. 436.
50. Ibid.
51. Ibid. See Jerome Landfield's fine analytical comments on all Sheridan's Begum speeches in the doctoral dissertation cited above in note 2.
52. Sadler, pp. 22 - 23.

Chapter Two

1. Sichel, I, 266.
2. The phrases quoted here come from Sichel's transcription of the manuscript. See Sichel, I, 265 - 66.
3. *Plays and Poems of Richard Brinsley Sheridan*, ed. R. Crompton Rhodes (New York, 1962), III, 110. Afterwards cited as *Plays and Poems*. Except where otherwise noted, this edition supplies the texts of Sheridan's poems.
4. Both Walter Sichel and Crompton Rhodes credit Sheridan with this poem. Rhodes defends the attribution in *Plays and Poems*, III, 169 - 72.
5. The canons of common sense are emphasized in Sheridan's note (*Plays and Poems*, III, 190) analyzing the grammar of several of Sancho's lines.

Here Sheridan further insists that in slight poems, "where there are no *very* violent flights of Imagination to draw one's attention from the inferior articles of Sense and Grammar . . . correctness and perspicacity are points never to be dispensed with."

6. *Plays and Poems*, III, 137.

7. Ibid., 137 and 139.

8. Sichel, I, 290.

9. *Plays and Poems*, III, 137.

10. J. W. Draper, "The Theory of Translation in the Eighteenth Century," *Neophilologus*, VI (1921), 254.

11. *Plays and Poems*, III, 139.

12. Cf. Jonson's "Still to Be Neat" from *Epicoene*, Herrick's "Delight in Disorder."

13. "Simplicity, A Changing Concept," *Journal of the History of Ideas* XIV (1953), 18. *Spectator* #85.

14. Marjorie L. Barstow Greenbie, *Wordsworth's Theory of Poetic Diction* (New York, 1966), p. 61.

15. *Plays and Poems*, III, 139.

16. Greenbie, p. 61, quoting Goldsmith's *Life of Thomas Parnell*.

17. Ibid., pp. 61 - 62.

18. *Plays and Poems*, III, 141.

19. Ibid., 146.

20. Thomas Sheridan, *A Course of Lectures on Elocution* (London, 1762), pp. 165 - 66.

21. *Plays and Poems*, III, 139.

22. See A. Bosker, *Literary Criticism in the Age of Johnson* (New York, 1953), p. 117.

23. See Bosker, p. 166 (for Alexander Gerard's definition of taste), p. 189 (for Hugh Blair's definition), p. 201 (for James Beattie's), p. 162 (for Hume's). Cf. Sheridan's admiration in "A Familiar Epistle" for those who "give to reason, reason's due" and "in the volume of the brain, / Reserve to Taste one candid page" (178).

24. Bosker, pp. 115 and 137 (for Johnson and Kames on Common Sense).

25. See Bosker, p. 123. Also see Redding S. Sugg, Jr., "The Mood of Eighteenth-Century Grammar," *Philological Quarterly*, XLIII (1964), 239 - 52.

26. For a discussion of the esthetic supporting Sheridan's judgment, see Dean Tolle Mace, "The Doctrine of Sound and Sense in Augustan Poetic Theory," *Review of English Studies*, new series. II (1951), 129 - 39.

27. Bosker, p. 101, documents this general view by citing Samuel Johnson's *Life of Waller*: "Poetry pleases by exhibiting an idea more grateful to the mind than things themselves afford."

28. In "A Familiar Epistle" (p. 179), Sheridan urges poetry to catch the pencil from Nature's hand and "with a bold, creative line, / Deserve the title of *divine*." In "The Tendency Toward Platonism in Neo-Classical

Esthetics," *English Literary History*, I (1934), 91 - 119, Louis Bredvold explains André Félibien's neo-Platonic theory of imitation as follows: "Art . . . is divine, a sort of human analogue to the all-mighty power of God, who created the universe out of nothing" (102 - 103).

29. For the rationalist view see J. W. H. Atkins, *English Literary Criticism: 17th and 18th Centuries* (London, 1951), pp. 281; 288 - 89. Also see Wallace C. Brown, *Charles Churchill: Poet, Rake, Rebel* (Lawrence, Kansas, 1953), p. 206, where contemporary strictures against Churchill's satiric poetry directly parallel those against satire in "A Familiar Epistle," p. 186.

30. See Bosker, p. 212, citing Joseph Warton's condemnation of Pope's satires. The reasons for Warton's reservations directly reflect those given by Sheridan in "A Familiar Epistle," pp. 194 - 96.

31. Cf. "Clio's Protest," p. 118 and "A Familiar Epistle," p. 196.

32. See Chester F. Chapin, *Personification in Eighteenth-Century English Poetry* (New York, 1955), pp. 59 - 61, for a discussion of personification in relation to conventional expectation. See Bosker, p. 102 for the conservative rationalist's view of particularity; see Chapin, p. 35, for the imaginationist view as expressed by Warton. Sheridan's view seems really that of the more liberal rationalist, as discussed by Scott Elledge in "The Background and Development in English Criticism of the Theories of Generality and Particularity," *Publications of the Modern Language Association*, LXII (1947), 177.

33. Paul Fussell, *Theory of Prosody in Eighteenth-Century England* (New London, Conn., 1954), p. 103.

34. Fussell (pp. 1 - 36) places the syllabist doctrine in historical context.

35. Ibid., pp. 124; 126.

36. Ibid., pp. 58; 64.

37. See Mace, p. 134 for mention of such theorists.

38. J. W. Draper, "Poetry and Music in Eighteenth Century Aesthetics," *Englische Studien*, LXVII (1932), 84.

39. Ibid., 84; 71, n. 1.

40. E. g., Brown *A Dissertation on . . . Poetry and Music* (1763) and Daniel Webb, *Observations on . . . Poetry and Music* (1769).

41. John Rice, *Introduction to the Art of Reading with Energy and Propriety* (London, 1765), cited in Fussell, p. 127.

42. Fussell, pp. 8; 133 - 57.

43. Except where otherwise noted, page references to the prologues and epilogues cite Volume III of *Plays and Poems*.

44. Colman's prologue to the opening of the Haymarket Theatre (1786) expresses this same view, as do others. See Mary Etta Knapp, *Prologues and Epilogues of the Eighteenth Century* (New Haven, 1961), pp. 268 - 69.

45. See Knapp, p. 273.

46. Ibid., pp. 262; 271.

47. *Plays and Poems*, I, 27.

48. Ibid., 28.

49. Sheridan's prologue goes counter to the received practice of support-ing Jonsonian satire in the prologues and epilogues of the century. See Knapp, p. 233.

50. See Knapp, pp. 197; 204; 266.

51. *Plays and Poems*, II, 218. Parenthetical page references to *The Critic* cite this volume.

52. As itemized, Puff's "rules" appear on the following pages of Rhodes's text of *The Critic:* (1) p. 235; (2) p. 229; (3) p. 231; (4) p. 228; (5) p. 225.

Chapter Three

1. Martin S. Day, "Anstey and Anapestic Satire in the Late Eighteenth Century," *English Literary History*, XV (1948), 128. Cecil Price attributes "Hymen and Hirco" to Sheridan in the *Times Literary Supplement* for July 11, 1958, p. 396.

2. Except where otherwise noted, page references to Sheridan's poetry cite Volume III of *Plays and Poems*.

3. These are Sichel's judgments (I, 314).

4. Ernest Rhys, *Lyric Poetry* (London, 1913), p. 370.

5. Sichel, I, 272.

6. As quoted in *A Vers de Société Anthology*, ed. Carolyn Wells (New York, 1907), p. xxiii.

7. Moore, I, 40 - 41.

8. Sichel, I, 273.

9. Ibid., 274; *Plays and Poems*, III, 229.

10. *Plays and Poems*, III, 259.

11. Moore, II, 90.

12. *Plays and Poems*, III, 197.

13. [15 Oct., 1814?], *Letters*, III, 202.

14. *Plays and Poems*, III, 198.

15. Sichel, I, 551.

16. Wallace Cable Brown, *The Triumph of Form* (Chapel Hill, 1948), p. 5.

17. Geoffrey Tillotson, *On the Poetry of Pope* (Oxford, 1950), p. 150.

18. Paul Fussell, *Theory of Prosody in Eighteenth-Century England*, (New London, Conn., 1954), pp. 113 - 15.

19. See the beginning of Chapter 2 above. For a much fuller discussion of Sheridan's prosody in relation to the theory of tensions see Jack D. Durant, "R. B. Sheridan's 'Verses to the Memory of Garrick': Poetic Reading as For-mal Theatre," *Southern Speech Journal*, XXXV (1969), 120 - 31.

20. Thomas Sheridan, *Lectures on the Art of Reading* (London, 1775), II, 75.

21. As quoted by Fussell, p. 113.

22. MS W. b. 479 (p. 133) in the Folger Shakespeare Library, a newspaper clipping not identified as to source (but bearing the handwritten date May 12, 1779), specifies the points at which musical interludes occur.

23. Quoting the second issue of the poem (one of several copies in the Folger collection), identical to the first except for a correction in the dedicatory epistle. A definitive text is now readily available in *The Dramatic Works of Richard Brinsley Sheridan*, ed. Cecil Price (Oxford, 1973), II, 457 - 62.

24. Moore, I, 176.

25. Thomas Sheridan, *Art of Reading*, II, 145.

26. Ibid., 84.

27. *Town and Country Magazine*, XI (1779), 117.

28. *The London Stage*, Pt. 5, Vol. 1, records performances at Drury Lane as follows: March 11, 13, 18, 20, 25; April 10, 21, 26; May 24; June 3.

29. George Gordon, Lord Byron, *Letters and Journals*, ed. Rowland E. Prothero (London, 1898), II, 377. For an expanded version of this discussion of the monody, see Jack D. Durant, "R. B. Sheridan's 'Verses to the Memory of Garrick': Poetic Reading as Formal Theatre," *Southern Speech Journal*, xxxv (1969), 120 - 31.

30. Knapp, p. 8.

31. Ibid., p. 28.

32. Cecil Price, in "The First Prologue to *The Rivals*," *Review of English Studies*, new series, XX (1969), 192 - 95, prints the fragmentary first-night prologue as recently found at Somerville College, Oxford.

33. Such changes were not unusual. See Knapp, p. 2.

34. See Knapp, pp. 278 - 79.

35. January 10 [1778], *Letters*, I, 122.

36. For comment on this persistent theme see Knapp, pp. 178; 185.

37. Second-night prologue to *The Rivals (Plays and Poems*, I, 25, 26); epilogue to *The Fatal Falsehood (Plays and Poems*, III, 275 - 77). See Knapp, p. 25; 96 - 97.

38. Second-night prologue to *The Rivals;* cf. Knapp, p. 108 for precedents.

39. Epilogue to *Edward and Eleanora;* cf. Knapp, p. 136 for precedents.

40. *Plays and Poems*, I, 27.

41. See Knapp, pp. 307 - 308.

42. *Plays and Poems*, III, 277.

Chapter Four

1. The most thorough and closely documented discussion of the first-night reception of *The Rivals* appears in the "Introduction" to the Larpent version of *The Rivals* as edited by Richard Little Purdy (Oxford, 1935), especially pp. xii - xviii. *The London Stage* (Part 4, Vol. 3, p. 1863) indicates that the play was indeed performed on the eighteenth and withdrawn after the second performance.

2. The revisions noted here all appear in Purdy, where the texts of the Larpent MS and the First Edition of 1775 are printed in parallel columns.

3. According to Sheridan's letter to Thomas Linley, November 17, 1774, *Letters*, I, 85.

4. Purdy, p. xli. For further information about texts, see *The Dramatic Works of Richard Brinsley Sheridan*, ed. Cecil Price (Oxford, 1973), I, 55 - 66.

5. *Plays and Poems*, I, 20. Parenthetical page references to the play and its epilogue cite this edition.

6. Ibid., I, 120.

7. P. Fijn van Draat, "Sheridan's *Rivals* and Ben Jonson's *Every Man in His Humour*," *Neophilologus*, XVIII (1933), 46.

8. Jean Dulck, *Les Comédies de Sheridan* (Paris, 1962), p. 115.

9. Miriam Gabriel and Paul Mueschke, "Two Contemporary Sources of Sheridan's *The Rivals*," *Publications of the Modern Language Association*, XLIII (1928), 237 - 40.

10. Sailendra Kumar Sen, "Sheridan's Literary Debt: *The Rivals* and *Humphry Clinker*," *Modern Language Quarterly*, XXI (1960), 294 - 300.

11. Gabriel and Mueschke, pp. 244 - 45, citing Ernest Bernbaum, *The Drama of Sensibility* (Boston, 1915), p. 352; and Sichel, I, 490.

12. J. Q. Adams, "Sources of *The Rivals*," in his introduction to *The Rivals* (Boston, 1910), p. xxi. But see G. H. Nettleton, *Sheridan's Major Dramas* (Boston, 1906), p. lvi.

13. Gabriel and Mueschke, p. 246.

14. Ibid., pp. 249 - 50.

15. Rhodes, *Harlequin*, pp. 56 - 57. Rhodes suggests that in attempting to revise his mother's play Sheridan added these details himself, in effect plagiarizing his own work.

16. Adams, p. xv. Dulck (pp. 448 - 51) offers an analysis of Mrs. Malaprop's language comparable to the one given in the foregoing section of this chapter.

17. Otto Reinert, ed. *An Anthology of Drama* (Boston, 1964), p. 386.

18. Adams, p. xvi; Reinert, p. 386.

19. Nettleton, *Major Dramas*, p. xl.

20. Allan Rodway, "Goldsmith and Sheridan: Satirists of Sentiment," *Renaissance and Modern Essays Presented to Vivian de Sola Pinto in Celebration of His Seventieth Birthday* (London, 1966), p. 70.

21. John Jeffrey, "*The Rivals* and *The School for Scandal*," *Edinburgh Review*, XLV (1826), 7.

22. George H. Niederauer, "Wit and Sentiment in Sheridan's Comedies of Manners" (Unpublished Ph. D. Dissertation, University of Southern California, 1966), p. 192 and throughout.

23. Ibid., p. 194.

24. Louis Kronenberger, *The Thread of Laughter* (New York, 1952), p. 193; Adams, p. xv.

25. Dulck, p. 356; Ashley Thorndike, *English Comedy* (New York, 1929), p. 433.

26. See J. O. Bartley, "The Development of a Stock Character: I, The Stage Irishman to 1800," *Modern Language Review*, XXXVII (1942), 445.

27. See Adams, p. xix; Thorndike, p. 431.

28. Rose Snider, *Satire in the Comedies of Congreve, Sheridan, Wilde, and Coward* (Orono, Maine. University of Maine Studies, 2nd Series, No. 42, 1937).

29. Arthur Sherbo, *English Sentimental Drama* (East Lansing, Mich., 1957), p. 85.

30. Leigh Hunt, *Dramatic Criticism, 1808 - 1831,* ed. Lawrence Huston Houtchens and Carolyn Washburn Houtchens (New York, 1949), p. 249.

31. Niederauer, p. 84.

32. Nettleton, *Major Dramas,* pp. xlix - l.

33. Ibid., pp. 323 - 4.

34. Reinert, p. 387.

35. Sen, p. 300.

36. Reinert, p. 383.

37. Aubrey De Selincourt, *Six Great Playwrights* (London, 1960), p. 117.

38. Reinert, p. 385.

39. Ibid.

40. Snider, p. 47.

41. Niederauer, p. 83.

42. H. T. E. Perry, *Masters of Dramatic Comedy and Their Social Themes* (Cambridge, Mass., 1939), p. 278; Reinert, p. 385; Niederauer, p. 162.

43. Moore, I, 88 - 91; Rae, I, 269 - 74.

44. Sichel, I, 467; Oscar Sherwin, *Uncorking Old Sherry* (London, 1960), pp. 113 - 14.

45. *Letters,* I, 85.

46. The epilogue was first published in the *Town and Country Magazine,* VII (February, 1775), 103 - 104. Quotations from the epilogue cite *Plays and Poems,* I, 114 - 15.

47. Parenthetical page references cite Cecil Price's edition of the "Sanctuary" in Sheridan's *Letters,* I, 47 - 59.

48. Brackets here and elsewhere in the "Sanctuary" are Price's.

49. "Three illegible words," as Price indicates, obscure Sheridan's precise plan for *The Whole Duty of Man;* but the contexts suggest he intended close study of it. Lydia, it will be recalled, orders *The Innocent Adultery* hidden inside *The Whole Duty of Man* (I, 2, p. 37). Contemporary criticism of Lydia's novels is quoted by Nettleton (in *Major Dramas,* p. lxxi and lxxii). Sheridan's letter to Thomas Grenville for October 30, 1772, *Letters,* I, 61, clarifies his distinction between novels and romances.

50. Dulck, p. 119.

51. John Philip Kemble records the tradition in a prompt-book copy of the play to be used in the season 1803 - 1804. See Purdy, p. li.

52. Bernbaum, p. 253.

53. Sherbo, p. 102.

54. In somewhat different form this discussion of the "form and meaning" of the play appears in Jack D. Durant, "Sheridan's 'Royal Sanctuary': A Key to *The Rivals,*" *Ball State University Forum,* XIV (Winter, 1973), 23 - 30.

Chapter Five

1. See, for example, the *London Magazine*, XLIV (December, 1775), 611; *Monthly Review*, LIII (December, 1775), 518; *Oxford Magazine*, XII, (November, 1775), 343; *Town and Country*, VII (November, 1775), 603.

2. Detailed discussions of English comic opera drawn upon here include Edward Joseph Dent, *Foundations of English Opera* (New York, 1965); Edmond M. Gagey, *Ballad Opera* (New York, 1937); W. J. Lawrence, "Early Irish Ballad Opera and Comic Opera," *The Musical Quarterly*, VIII (July, 1922), 397 - 412; Allardyce Nicoll, *A History of Late Eighteenth-Century Drama*, 1750 - 1800 (Cambridge, England, 1927); and William Eben Schultz, *Gay's Beggar's Opera: Its Content, History, and Influence* (New Haven, 1923).

3. Sources for *The Duenna* are suggested in Dulck, pp. 152 - 54; Sichel, I, 505 - 506; Moore, I, 113; Nicoll, p. 205; *Plays and Poems*, I, 181.

4. See Dulck, pp. 161; 153.

5. Martin Armstrong, " 'The Duenna' and 'The Pelican,' " *Spectator*, CXXXIII (November, 1924), 637.

6. F. S. Boas, *An Introduction to Eighteenth-Century Drama, 1700 - 1780* (Oxford, 1953), p. 351; *Plays and Poems*, I, 181.

7. Brander Matthews, " 'Pinafore's Predecessor,' " *Harper's Magazine*, LX (1879 - 80), 504.

8. Moore, I, 115.

9. Sichel, I, 505.

10. Roger Fiske, "A Score for 'The Duenna,' " *Music and Letters*, XLII (April, 1961), 138 - 41.

11. Fiske, pp. 136 - 37.

12. In *Plays and Poems*, I, 249.

13. See Fiske, p. 134.

14. *Letters*, I, 86 - 88.

15. Ibid., 88 - 90.

16. Ibid., 90 - 92.

17. Moore, I, 116 - 18; Sichel, I, 509.

18. Dulck, pp. 157 - 60.

19. *The Radio Times*, July 17, 1953, as quoted by Dulck, pp. 154 - 55.

20. William Hazlitt, "On the Comic Writers of the Last Century," in *The Complete Works of William Hazlitt*, ed. P. P. Howe (London, 1931), VI, 165.

Chapter Six

1. Moore, I, 159. Cecil Price, in "Sheridan's 'Doxology,' " *Times Literary Supplement*, May 4, 1962, p. 309, provides what is probably the authentic text.

2. Sichel, I, 564. In *The Dramatic Works of Richard Brinsley Sheridan*, I,

289, Cecil Price suggests that Samuel Foote's *The Maid of Bath* (1771) gave Sheridan "some initial ideas and situations" for *The School for Scandal.*

3. *Plays and Poems*, II, 128.

4. Moore, I, 145.

5. *Plays and Poems*, II, 135.

6. Ibid. 141.

7. Dulck, pp. 216 - 17.

8. Christian Deelman, "The Original Cast of *The School for Scandal*," *Review of English Studies*, XIII (1962), 257 - 66.

9. Moore, I, 164.

10. Thorndike, p. 435.

11. Louis Kronenberger, *The Thread of Laughter* (New York, 1952), pp. 200 - 201.

12. Cleanth Brooks and Robert Heilman, *Understanding Drama: Twelve Plays* (New York, 1948), pp. 249 - 50.

13. Henry James, "*The School for Scandal* at Boston," *Scenic Art: Notes on Acting and the Drama, 1872 - 1901,* ed. Allan Wade (New York, 1957), p. 17.

14. Niederauer, p. 140.

15. Prosser Hall Frye, *Visions and Chimeras* (Boston, 1929), p. 13.

16. Andrew Schiller, "*The School for Scandal:* The Restoration Unrestored," *Publications of the Modern Language Association*, LXXI (1956), 703.

17. Brooks and Heilman, p. 245.

18. William Hazlitt, *Complete Works*, V, 291.

19. Schiller, p. 699.

20. Brooks Atkinson, "Sheridan — Whom the Gods Loved," in *Essays of Today (1926 - 27),* ed. O. Shepherd and R. S. Hillyer (New York, 1928), p. 371.

21. J. R. de J. Jackson, "The Importance of Witty Dialogue in *The School for Scandal,*" *Modern Language Notes*, LXXVI (1961), 601 - 607. See Sichel, I, 571.

22. Moore, I, 163.

23. Schiller, p. 699.

24. G. H. Nettleton, *English Drama of the Restoration and Eighteenth Century* (New York, 1928), pp. 303 - 304.

25. R. S. Crane, "Suggestions toward a Genealogy of the 'Man of Feeling'," *English Literary History*, I (1934), 224.

26. Cornell, 1965, pp. 244 - 67.

27. Kronenberger, p. 196.

28. Crane, 225, quoting sermons by Z. Isham (1700), William Dawes (1708), and Richard Fiddes (1720).

29. Brooks and Heilman, p. 253.

30. Parenthetical references cite Volume II of *Plays and Poems.*

31. Dulck, pp. 202 - 203. Dulck calls the scene a little comedy in *four* acts.
32. Moore, I, 155.
33. Sichel, I, 555.
34. Portions of this discussion of *The School for Scandal* appear also in Jack D. Durant, "The Moral Focus of *The School for Scandal*," *South Atlantic Bulletin*, XXXVII (November, 1972), 44 - 53.

Chapter Seven

1. V. C. Clinton-Baddeley, *The Burlesque Tradition in the English Theatre after 1660* (London, 1952), p. 72. Baddeley also discusses *The Critic* in relation to Fielding's burlesque (pp. 52, 62, 63), and Dane Farnsworth Smith, in *The Critics in the Audience of the London Theatres from Buckingham to Sheridan* (Albuquerque, 1953), pp. 122 - 27, compares *The Critic* to Colman's *New Brooms*. Crompton Rhodes, in *Plays and Poems*, II, 181, discusses *The Critic* in relation to Garrick's *Peep Behind the Curtain*. Rhodes also reprints portions of the burletta *Ixion* (II, 245 - 49), seeing it as a forerunner of *The Critic*.
2. *Plays and Poems*, II, 181.
3. Smith, p. 129.
4. Sichel, I, 605.
5. Ibid.
6. These echoes are noted and discussed in many places, e. g., *Plays and Poems*, II, 185, 186, 187; Nettleton, *Eighteenth Century Drama*, p. 310; Moore, I, 180 - 81; Smith, p. 142.
7. The most extensive discussion of *The Critic* in relation to *The Rehearsal* appears in Dulck, pp. 262 - 69. See more generalized comments in Smith, pp. 141 - 42; Baddeley, pp. 31; 178 - 79.
8. Dulck, p. 274.
9. Baddeley, p. 74.
10. Ibid., p. 75.
11. Smith, p. 127.
12. Dulck, p. 249.
13. Parenthetical page references cite Volume II of *Plays and Poems*.
14. Ibid., 259.
15. See A. Loewenberg, "The Songs in 'The Critic,' " *Times Literary Supplement*, March 28, 1942, p. 168.
16. See *Plays and Poems*, II, 179.
17. Ibid., 244.
18. Rhodes, *Harlequin*, p. 85.

Chapter Eight

1. See *Plays and Poems*, III, 295; Sichel, II, 265.
2. *Plays and Poems*, III, 297. But see *The Dramatic Works of Richard Brinsley Sheridan*, ed. Cecil Price (Oxford, 1973), II, 810, Price sees *Affectation* as begun possibly as early as 1772 - 73.
3. See Moore, I, 212 - 13; *Plays and Poems*, III, 298.

4. As quoted in *Plays and Poems,* III, 303.

5. Ibid., 307. In his bibliography of Sheridan's works, Sichel draws no relationship between "A Wild Drama" and the sketch based on "The Goblins." See Sichel, II, 458.

6. *Plays and Poems,* III, 309.

7. Ibid., 310.

8. Michael Kelly, *Reminiscences* (New York, 1969), p. 344. (First issued in 1826).

9. The phrase is Moore's, I, 19. Moore prints generous portions of the manuscript (I, 19 - 22).

10. Ibid., 19.

11. Sichel, I, 297.

12. Moore, I, 22, 23.

13. See Sichel, I, 443; II, 459; I, 22; I, 34; II, 454. See Price, *The Dramatic Works of Richard Brinsley Sheridan,* II, 775 - 845.

14. On the attribution see Moore, I, 174; Sichel, I, 443; Rhodes, *Plays and Poems,* II, 271 - 72; pp. 305 - 306. Also see George W. Williams, "A New Source of Evidence for Sheridan's Authorship of *The Camp* and *The Wonders of Derbyshire,*" *Studies in Philology,* XLVII (1950), 619 - 28. Sheridan's authorship of *The Wonders of Derbyshire* is not widely credited.

15. Dulck, p. 300.

16. According to Rhodes, *Plays and Poems,* III, 316.

17. Moore, II, 187 - 88. The text of *The Glorious First of June* is now available in *The Dramatic Works of Richard Brinsley Sheridan,* ed. Cecil Price (Oxford, 1973), II, 759 - 74.

18. Moore, II, 203.

19. Myron Matlaw, "*Menschenhass und Reue* in English," *Symposium,* XIV (1960), 131 - 32.

20. Regarding Schink's submission see Matlaw, *Menschenhass,* 130.

21. *Plays and Poems,* III, 311.

22. John Genest, *Some Account of the English Stage* (Bath, 1832), VII, 707.

23. Moore, II, 188.

24. For historical background see *Plays and Poems,* III, 311.

25. Ibid., 312.

26. Ibid., 337.

27. To Lady Ossory, Sunday, November 3, 1782, in *The Yale Edition of Horace Walpole's Correspondence,* ed. W. S. Lewis (New Haven, 1965), XXXIII, 361.

28. *European Magazine,* I (February, 1782), 80.

29. See G. H. Nettleton, "Sheridan's *Robinson Crusoe,*" *Times Literary Supplement,* June 23, 1945, p. 300. According to *The London Stage* (Part 5, Volume I, p. clxxiii), *Crusoe* was performed 123 times between 1781 and 1800. In *The Dramatic Works of Richard Brinsley Sheridan,* II, 787, Cecil Price offers the possibility that Mrs. Sheridan wrote *Crusoe.*

30. *London Stage* records performances on May 6, 9, 15, 25; June 1.

31. "The British Theatre," *London Magazine*, XLIV (1774), 242.

32. Rhodes, *Harlequin*, pp. 68 - 69.

33. *Plays and Poems*, I, 281.

34. Jeremy Collier, "A Short View of the Immorality and Profaneness of the English Stage," in *English Literary Criticism: Restoration and 18th Century*, ed. Samuel Hynes (New York, 1963), pp. 97 - 130.

35. Dulck, p. 167.

36. According to Rhodes *(Harlequin*, p. 69).

37. Ibid., 182.

38. See Myron Matlaw, "English Versions of *Die Spanier in Peru*," *Modern Language Quarterly*, XVI (1955), 63.

39. Myron Matlaw, " 'This Is Tragedy!!!' The History of *Pizarro*," *Quarterly Journal of Speech*, XLIII (1957), 289. Matlaw discusses the immense popularity of the piece.

40. See Grzegorz Sinko, *Sheridan and Kotzebue* (Wroclaw, 1949), p. 12. But see also Cecil Price's discussion of the translation in *The Dramatic Works of Richard Brinsley Sheridan*, II, 645 - 46.

41. About the payments made to secure his basic text, see Rhodes, *Harlequin*, pp. 176 - 77; about the translator, see Sinko, p. 12.

42. See Sinko, p. 12. Sinko's careful study provides much of the comparative detail given in my own discussion. Rhodes remarks (in *Harlequin*, p. 182) that the prodigious length of the play was abridged "after the first few nights" probably by John Philip Kemble.

43. Moore, II, 212, indicates that other of Sheridan's speeches also fleshed the fustian of *Pizarro*, significantly the speeches on invasion spoken before the Commons in 1799.

44. Moore, I, 211.

45. See Rhodes, *Harlequin*, pp. 181 - 82. The story originates with Daniel Stuart, the proprietor of *The Courier*.

46. R. B. Sheridan, "Sheridan Against Warren Hastings on the Begum Charge," in *Select British Eloquence*, ed. Chauncey H. Goodrich (New York, 1963), p. 425.

47. Ibid.

48. Ibid.

49. Ernest Bernbaum, *The Drama of Sensibility* (Boston, 1915), Chapter XIII.

50. Mark S. Auburn, footnote #2 of "The Pleasures of Sheridan's *The Rivals:* A Critical Study in the Light of Stage History," forthcoming in *Modern Philology*. The author is grateful to Professor Auburn for making this essay available to him before its publication.

51. George C. D. Odell, in *Annals of the New York Stage* (New York, 1927 - 49), records at least 433 performances of *The School for Scandal* between 1785 and 1894.

Selected Bibliography

BIBLIOGRAPHIES

SICHEL, WALTER. "Bibliography of Sheridan's Works Published and Unpublished." In *Sheridan from New and Original Sources*. London: Constable, 1909. Vol. II. Appendix V. 445 - 59.

WILLIAMS, IOLO A. *Seven XVIIIth Century Bibliographies*. London: Dulau, 1924.

PRIMARY SOURCES

BOND, E. A. *Speeches of the Managers and Counsel in the Trial of Warren Hastings*. 4 vols. London: 1859 - 61. Best reported text of Sheridan's Westminster Hall speech.

NETTLETON, G. H. *The Major Dramas of Richard Brinsley Sheridan, with an Introduction*. Boston: Ginn, 1906. Contains *Rivals, School* and *Critic*.

PRICE, CECIL J. B. *The Dramatic Works of Richard Brinsley Sheridan*. 2 vols. Oxford: The Clarendon Press, 1973. Excellent scholarly edition; careful, thorough, closely and extensively documented.

———. *The Letters of Richard Brinsley Sheridan*. 3 vols. Oxford: The Clarendon Press, 1966.

RHODES, R. CROMPTON. *The Plays and Poems of Richard Brinsley Sheridan*. Oxford: Blackwell, 1928. Extensive bibliographic notes.

The Speeches of the Right Honourable Richard Brinsley Sheridan. With a Sketch of His Life. Edited by a Constitutional Friend. 3 vols. New York: Russell and Russell, 1969. First issued in 1842; differs only in punctuation and spelling from five-volume issue of 1816.

SECONDARY SOURCES

1. Biography

MOORE, THOMAS. *Memoirs of the Life of the Right Honourable Richard Brinsley Sheridan*. London: [Longman], 1825. First biography to be based upon proper documents and sources.

RAE, W. FRASER. *Sheridan: A Biography*. 2 vols. New York: Holt, 1896. Commissioned by the Sheridan family to expand and correct Moore.

RHODES, R. CROMPTON. *Harlequin Sheridan: The Man and the Legends.*

Oxford: Blackwell, 1933. Brisk, authoritative scholarly account of the highlights of Sheridan's life.

SADLER, MICHAEL T. H. *The Political Career of R. B. Sheridan.* Oxford: Blackwell, 1912. Still the best analytical account of Sheridan's political career. Recently reissued by Darby Reprints.

SICHEL, WALTER. *Sheridan from New and Original Sources.* 2 vols. London: Constable, 1909. Exhaustive, closely documented; provides generous extracts from Sheridan's juvenilia.

2. Criticism (literary and historical background, interpretation, and analysis)

BROOKS, CLEANTH and ROBERT B. HEILMAN (eds.). *Understanding Drama: Twelve Plays.* New York: Holt, 1948. Very close critical reading of *The School for Scandal.*

DEELMAN, CHRISTIAN. "The Original Cast of *The School for Scandal,*" *Review of English Studies,* xiii)1962), 257 - 66. Important essay; shows that Sheridan shaped his characters to fit hs cast.

DULCK, JEAN. *Les Comédies de Sheridan.* Paris: Didier, 1962. Careful, thorough study of Sheridan's comedies and his comic art. Quite fine.

DURANT, JACK D. "Prudence, Providence, and the Direct Road of Wrong: *The School for Scandal* and Sheridan's Westminster Hall Speech," *Studies in Burke and His Time,* XV (1974), 241 - 51. The speech is a "moral analogue" of the play.

FIJN VAN DRAAT, P. "Sheridan's *Rivals* and Ben Jonson's *Every Man in His Humour,*" *Neophilologus,* XVIII (1933), 44 - 50. Points out parallels in characterization.

FISKE, ROGER. "A Score for 'The Duenna'," *Music and Letters,* XLII (April, 1961), 132 - 41. Identifies composers, melodies, orchestrations, and ornamentations. Valuable article.

GABRIEL, MIRIAM and PAUL MUESCHKE. "Two Contemporary Sources of Sheridan's *The Rivals,*" *Publications of the Modern Language Association,* XLIII (1928), 237 - 50. Garrick's *Miss in Her Teens* and Colman's *The Deuce Is in Him.*

JACKSON, J. R. DE J. "The Importance of Witty Dialogue in *The School for Scandal,*" *Modern Language Notes,* LXXXVI (1961), 601 - 607. Sees Sheridan constructing *The School for Scandal* so as to save the best witty sallies from the fragments of the play.

KRONENBERGER, LOUIS. *The Thread of Laughter: Chapters on English Stage Comedy from Jonson to Maugham.* New York: Alfred A. Knopf, 1952. Describes the quality of Sheridan's comedy in relation to changing comic traditions.

LANDFIELD, JEROME BLANCHARD. "The Triumph and Failure of Sheridan's Speeches against Hastings," *Speech Monographs,* XXVIII (1961), 143 - 56. Drawn from Landfield's careful and thorough Ph.D. thesis on this subject (Missouri, 1959).

LEFF, LEONARD, J. "The Disguise Motif in Sheridan's *The School for Scan-*

dal," *Educational Theatre Journal*, XXII (1970), 350 - 60. Sees the motif of disguise as a major unifying feature of the play.

LOEWENBERG, A. "The Songs in *The Critic*," *Times Literary Supplement*, March 28, 1942, p. 168. Comments on composers, music, and lyrics.

LUTAUD, OLIVER. "Des acharniens d'Aristophane au critique de Sheridan," *Les Langues Modernes*, LX (1966), 433 - 38. Points up striking similarities in parodic strategies and serio-comic political ironies in *The Acharnians* of Aristophanes and Sheridan's *The Critic*.

MACMILLAN, DOUGALD. "Sheridan's Share in *The Stranger*," *Modern Language Notes*, XLV (1930), 85 - 86. Sheridan changes some names, adds vaudeville, and shortens the play.

MATLAW, MYRON. "Adultery Analyzed: The History of *The Stranger*," *Quarterly Journal of Speech*, XLIII (1957), 22 - 28.

———. " 'This Is Tragedy!!!': The History of *Pizarro*," *Quarterly Journal of Speech*, XLIII (1957), 288 - 94.

NELSON, DAVID A. "The Laughing Comedy of the Eighteenth Century." Unpublished Ph.D. thesis (Cornell, 1965). Valuable analysis of the developing conventions of "laughing comedy."

NETTLETON, G. H. *Sheridan et les comédies de moeurs*. Paris: C. Lavrut, 1931. Lecture placing Sheridan's plays in the larger tradition of the comedy of manners.

———. "Sheridan's Introduction to the American Stage," *Publications of the Modern Language Association*, LXV (1950), 163 - 82. Earliest performances in this country identified by date, theater, and region.

NIEDERAUER, REV. GEORGE H. "Wit and Sentiment in Sheridan's Comedies of Manners." Unpublished Ph.D. thesis (Southern California, 1966). Sees developing mastery in Sheridan's management of witty, sentimental language.

PRICE, CECIL. "Sheridan at Work on *The Stranger*," *Neuphilologische Mitteilungen*, LXXIII (1972), 315 - 25. Reprints several scenes of *The Stranger*, showing Sheridan's interlineations in "the second stage of revision."

RODWAY, ALLAN. "Goldsmith and Sheridan: Satirists of Sentiment." *Renaissance and Modern Essays Presented to Vivian de Sola Pinto*. London: Routledge, 1965. Discusses the two playwrights as satirists of sentiment.

ROTHWELL, KENNETH S. "*The School for Scandal*: The Comic Spirit in Sheridan and Rowlandson." *School for Scandal: Thomas Rowlandson's London*. Lawrence: Kansas University Museum of Art, 1967. Sees *The School for Scandal* as emphasizing the balance between nature and art.

SCHILLER, ANDREW. "*The School for Scandal*: The Restoration Unrestored," *Publications of the Modern Language Association*, LXII (1956), 694 - 704. Explains Sheridan's accommodations to changing comic values.

SEN, SAILENDRA KUMAR. "Sheridan's Literary Debt: *The Rivals* and

Humphry Clinker," Modern Language Quarterly, XXI (1960), 291 - 300. Notes parallels in character and comedy.

SPRAGUE, ARTHUR C. "In Defense of a Masterpiece: *The School for Scandal* Reexamined," *English Studies Today.* Third Series. G. I. Duthie, ed. Edinburgh: Edinburgh University, 1964. Sees the continuing success of *The School for Scandal* to lie in its special properties as "an acting play and . . . a play for actors."

WILLIAMS, GEORGE W. "A New Source of Evidence for Sheridan's Authorship of *The Camp* and *The Wonders of Derbyshire," Studies in Philology,* XLVII (1950), 619 - 28. Finds evidence in the Drury Lane Account Books at the Folger Shakespeare Library.

YEARLING, ELIZABETH M. "The Good-Natured Heroes of Cumberland, Goldsmith, Sheridan," *Modern Language Review,* LXVII (1972), 490 - 500. Goldsmith and Sheridan attack not "sentimental philosophy" but "debased sentimentality."

Index

(The works of Sheridan are listed under his name)

161